To my darling Lydia and our amazing children,
Renaldo, Tehilla, Christo and Stefan

Mirror Word Logo by: Wilna Furstenburg

Cover Design by: Francois du Toit and Sean Osmond

Published by Mirror Word Publishing

Books by the same author: Mirror Bible, Divine Embrace, The Logic of His Love, The Mystery Revealed, The Triumph of Friendship, DONE!

Children's book, The Eagle Story, by Lydia and Francois du Toit, beautifully
illustrated by Carla Krige

Botoks also available on Kindle

Francois' ministry page is www.mirrorword.net

Subscribe to Francois facebook updates http://www.facebook.com/francois.toit

Friends of The Mirror www.mirrorfriends.com

The Mirror Translation fb grouphttp://www.facebook.com/groups/179109018883718/?fref=ts

ISBN 978-0-9921769-2-1

INDEX

PREFACE

Life sometimes seems to be like a mighty magnet, which compels one almost in remote control fashion.

Yet if karma has the final say, why would it appear that some people are luckier than others? Our own thoughts, words, choices, habits and attitudes continue to turn and empower circumstances, events and people, which in turn touch and shape our destiny. Yet we often find ourselves trapped in confusion where life no longer seems to make any sense.

I believe that within the horizon of our hearts, the voice of our spirit echoes truth. We are designed to explore and discover our inmost self, the wealth of light and life within our reach. Even the sense of hopelessness in a crisis would prompt us to dig deeper to find a rock-solid foundation inside of us.

I trust that this writing will challenge and stir you to the core of your being and your beliefs to remove every trace of the substitute, man-made self-image with its glorious head of golden glitter and its silvery bust and bronze body. The little stone that was cut out by no human hand is destined to strike that image of vanity and piety on its feet of iron and clay and become in its place a Rock that fills the whole earth; the true image and likeness of God, restored and revealed in ordinary human life. (Dan 2:32-35)

Col 4:4 My sincere desire is that my message will accurately unveil the mystery of Christ in its most complete context: You! This is the mission of my life!

WHALES AND THE SABI SAND

My family and I live in Hermanus, near Cape Town. This is certainly one of the most beautiful towns in South Africa, and famous for the world's best land-based whale watching.

The Southern Right Whale visits our bay every year between June and December to mate and calve. For many years Hermanus remained a quiet fishing- and holiday-village. But you cannot hide a 14-meter, 40-ton mammal forever. Certainly not up to 200 of them frolicking, breaching, spy hopping and lob-tailing galore!

We moved here seven years ago, (at the time of writing, 2002) after a most devastating crisis year. In 1996 our business, and almost our marriage, crashed. It felt as if we had fallen into a deep dark pit. Not only did I lose my father, but also one of our dearest friends died in a motorbike accident. For years nobody close to us, died. Suddenly, within a few months, six people whom we knew died in five separate light aircraft accidents. I crashed my own plane in the Sabi Sand Game Reserve, but crawled out of the wreck without a scratch. Yet they say any landing you can walk (or run) from is a good one! During that same year, we were introduced into a 'wonderful' investment opportunity, which turned out to be a pyramid-scheme. Millions of Rand were involved, and many people were badly hurt.

But for four years prior to this we lived our dream. I negotiated an agreement with one of the owners of a farm in the Sabi Sand Private Game Reserve, bordering the famous Kruger National Park. We designed, built and managed our own Bush Lodge with five en-suite double rooms. The camp was rustic and warm with ambience and character. While Lydia won the admiration of the guests with her cooking-talent on the open fire, my brother's son, Hanri and I entertained them with walking safaris. During weekends and school holidays our four children practiced their hospitality skills. Shinga was located in pure African paradise. This was certainly a time of fantastic experience and rich memory. We met wonderful people and shared unforgettable moments.

In 1996 I involved a partner who impressed the owner of the farm with his financial connections. We then reached an agreement to proceed with the upgrading of what would become one of the most luxurious lodges in the Sabi Sand. The plans for the new lodge were finalized and all advance bookings for Shinga were cancelled.

While on holiday in Rooi Els near Hermanus in December of 1996, we received news that shattered us: apparently the Sabi Sand Committee had rejected all our plans for the new lodge. We were further informed that we would not be allowed to re-open Shinga since the owners of the Sabi Sand decided to restrict the number of beds per farm. By now we had already discovered that we had lost everything in the investment scheme and, with the unexpected turn of events, we were forced to make sudden and dramatic decisions.

My mom and dad's parents as well as my father's grandparents lived in Hermanus for many years. We spent most of our holidays here. The 'De Wets-huis Museum' was my great-grandfather's house. He did not want to have his children study under an English teacher, so he imported Hemanus Pieters from Holland! He had farms in Worcester, Caledon and Greyton. The Western Cape have winter rains and the summers are often so dry that in those days the farmers were forced to trek with their livestock along the rivers to find better grazing. It was during one of those summer vacations that Hermanus Pieters followed the 'Elephant path" along the Onrust river and across the mountain tending my great grandfather's livestock. He discovered the most picturesque bay with plenty grazing and fresh water springs all along the coastline. News about this beautiful bay with its natural harbor and its massive schools of fish spread rapidly. It soon became custom for farmers to move to the area and spend their summers here, grazing their livestock and indulging in the abundant fish! The village was named after Hermanus Pieters. The lengthy name of "Hermanus Pieters Fontein" was later shortened to just Hermanus. Until the 1890's my great grand father operated six boats from the old harbor.

With our dreams shattered in the Sabi Sands it was not a difficult decision for us to relocate. The attraction of the sea and the possibility for our children to live in a town for the first time in their lives, with both the Primary and the High Schools a mere block away, helped us make up our minds.

In the meantime, 'back at the Ranch', the partner and the owner of the farm intercepted the plans for the new lodge. Since we were now living 2000 kilometers away from the bush, news about the new developments only reached us six months later via the grape-to-cape-vine.

But no one feels sorry for you if you live in Hermanus. And it does not even help to feel sorry for yourself. I tried for two years. I sulked and whined until Lydia one day observed that my conversation had become reduced to sighing. We were surrounded by exquisite natural beauty, and do we really have to own before we can enjoy? In fact we never really own anything in the material world beyond the fleeting moment or memory.

One day on my way to Cape Town to install swimming pool covers, a feeling of desperate hopelessness pressed upon me; nothing seemed to make sense any more. I had such a desire to just hear a voice that would somehow direct my confused thoughts. When I turned on the radio, I heard only one line of a song by Mike and the Mechanics, '…you're a beggar on a beach of gold!' Nothing you could ever lose can leave you feeling more poverty stricken and desolate than losing your awareness of the wealth within you.

What lies behind you and what lies before you are small matters compared to what lies within you. Ralph Waldo Emerson

For a decade I drifted in a wilderness of spiritual darkness and isolation. I started writing the notes that eventually triggered this book in December 2000. The whisper in the wind became a cloudburst of thought. My wish is that this study would be a lamp to the reader, especially for those going through a dark place. Anticipate the day to dawn for you as the morning star rises in your own heart. 2 Pet.1:19

GRAVITY

Everything begins somewhere. Sometimes it is difficult to trace the exact origin and moment, but you often suddenly become aware that you are caught up in the slipstream of something. You are either chasing something or something is chasing you. It reminds me of the story of a man who arrived out of breath and in a state of shock at a farmhouse. He had run away from a lion. The farmer asked him why he had not climbed into a tree... 'Huh! I was going too fast' he said.

Talking about a slipstream, a thought pattern often creates a momentum that forms a magnetic field with its own pull or gravity. Within a specific environment, the law of gravity works spontaneously. The nearer to the source, the more dynamic the effect of the law becomes. A thought often entertained becomes a footpath in the field of your imagination. A thought may remain secret and invisible for some time, but it inevitably will affect your conversation, your mood and your health. Your behaviour, whether it be your body language or attitude, will always betray your thoughts. An individual's attitude and mood can even transmit an invisible energy that influences others. How do we escape the habit of negative thinking? The mere effort to match a negative thought or even replace one with a positive thought can be most exhausting and often frustrating, leaving one with the feeling of fighting a losing battle. It becomes a vicious circle. Fighting depression this way can be more difficult than trying to quit cigarettes. We all know that light dispels darkness effortlessly, but how does one turn the light on? Is there a law that can counter the force of gravity?

When I trained for my pilot's licence, the instructor explained how the law of lift, in a sense, supersedes the law of gravity. One law neutralises the effect of another law, so to speak. To ultimately proceed beyond the atmosphere of the earth would bring about an experience of weightlessness. The law of gravity offers an interesting comparison to help understand how other laws work. A law does not work by chance. It does, however, work according to specific, predictable principles. Choice does not trigger the effect of gravity. Neither is gravity a respecter of persons; whether you are skinny, overweight, famous, attractive or poor, Catholic or Muslim, gravity will keep your feet on the ground; while you remain within the reach of its influence. But hey, you can always learn to fly! We tend to become so caught up and occupied within the immediate space of our day-to-day routine that we often neglect to discover the friend in our neighbour, beyond the concrete walls. Breaking through the boundaries of the known, to discover time and space in a different perspective and dimension, would certainly challenge the comfort-zone.

Science allows us to research our origin, and possible destiny, within the confined limits of what we perceive with our senses to be a realistic measure of space and time. This discipline, however, reaches a point where modern and sophisticated technology fails to calculate the infinite depth of our horizon.

The Hubble space-telescope captures images of the most breathtaking and colorful galaxies, millions of light years distant from us - the furthest the human eye has ever been able to pierce the skies. A light year measures the distance light travels at the astonishing speed of 300 000 kilometres per second over a period of one year! Should one be able to count just the stars in our galaxy at one star per second, it would take about 3000 years! And our galaxy is a relative little one amidst countless billions of others. Archaeologists patiently uncover fossils and skeletons from the dust and through carbon dating reveal historic evidence of millions of years ago. We continue to upgrade our methods and often make yesteryear's claims look ridiculous.

Fundamentally, all matter in the universe is made up of tiny separate particles called atoms. The nucleus of the atom is basically a sound wave, electrically charged, and vibrating spontaneously and continuously. A million times a million atoms make too small a lump to see, but with powerful microscopes we probe into this near-invisible world to unveil its secrets. We discover fascinating reflections of distance, energy and movement that mirror outer space. On scale, the distance between a whirling electron and the nucleus it revolves around within the atom, is further than the distance between the earth and the sun. (220 million kilometres!) Just when we hope to finally calculate the electron, it too breaks up into energy vibrations that blink in and out of our view millions of times per second.

To appreciate the comparative size of a an atom, the following illustrations will astound you: If one hundred and thirty libraries each contain eight million books, with one thousand pages, each page containing 50 000 dots, the sum total of the dots in these books would equal the number of atoms in one bubble of oxygen the size of a mustard seed! Or, imagine the smallest visible speck of soot divided amongst eight million people. Their mission in life would be to count the atoms present in their piece! If it were possible to count four atoms per second for eight hours a day, it would take them one hundred and fifty years to do!

The heavens cannot contain God yet his fullness is revealed in human form! Col 2:9,10. "We have this treasure in earthen vessels!" 2 Cor 4:7. In today's technology we appreciate the fact that a memory stick is not measured on the outside but that it is the inside that matters!

"Have you measured your heart? Have you measured the volume of your being? He has chosen you to accommodate the fullness of his dream. He knows you by name, his design is his claim." Anthea van der Pluym

Time measures the rhythm of constant change, moments become days, nights and seasons; the eternal frequency of life is registered here. From our exclusive perception of time, we risk definition to capture a glimpse of eternity; we probe space with blunt instruments, measuring speed and distance in our hungry quest for reason.

Where do we fit into this vast picture of space and time? Are we a mere afterthought of creation or are we in fact what creation is all about? Would God find an expression of his likeness in man that would ultimately intrigue him and fulfil his dream for companionship forever? God's eternal love dream realized in his image bearer man, gives context and relevance to the life of our design.

SPOOKY STUFF

Nothing is more fascinating than to witness windows of spirit within your reach, open beyond the blurry boundaries of the senses and science. The attraction promises the most rewarding encounter. Spirit knowledge unveils the invisible world of thought and imagination. Here, feedback is reduced to resonance, and conclusion is the fruit of faith. When tuning a stringed instrument, another string will spontaneously begin to vibrate when the exact pitch corresponds to it.

Humans have a built-in ability to discern truth. We have within us the distinct talent to appreciate value. This exceeds any persuasion or argument, and defeats doubt.

There is so much more to life than its visible expression in the meat-box. There is so much more to you than what meets the eye! Our appetite distinguishes us from the animal world. The statement that man shall not live by bread alone, suggests that enjoying a fulfilled life requires more than just the feeding of the flesh. Luke 4:4. Our inherent value-consciousness drives us to explore beyond our next harvest in our quest to find wisdom that would match our soul hunger. Job 28

Many affluent people today are totally dependent on anti-depressants. Wealth and fame certainly does not guarantee a fulfilled life! Instead, depression has become the modern illness. Yet, in a sense, we have never had it any better. Science has given us remarkable medical break-throughs to enable us to live longer and safer than ever before. There are more people alive today than the total number of people who ever died in the history of mankind. With the popular emphasis on healthy eating and exercise one should almost be able to live forever!

The entertainment of the senses has become the biggest industry of our times; whether it is the big-money-sport, film, music, drama, travel, or food and wine-thing, not even to mention religion or the drug and porn-industry. If ultimate fulfilment could be attained this way then people on the planet should be happiest now since the beginning of time. We bombard our senses with high definition information and sensation. We have never known more. We have never travelled faster. Our children astound us with their technological skills and we continue to challenge and better our best performances in every athletic discipline.

From the 1700s to the 1800s, the ends of the earth shrunk from six months' distance to six weeks. In the early 1900s this became a mere three days. My grandmother travelled from Cape Town to Pretoria the first time when she was six years old, by ox wagon. The adventurous round trip of about 3000 kilometres lasted many months. In 1961, when she was eighty, my father fetched her from Hermanus and they flew from Cape Town to Johannesburg in just over two hours! In that same decade man landed on the moon! Today we transport ourselves anywhere in the world in a few hours, and are globally in touch within split seconds. Even outer space could become a tourist destination!

Life has become so convenient. We have so much available to us at the mere touch of a button. Yet greed and a constant sense of lack seem to dominate both poor and rich. We have proved that we are not designed to live by bread alone, our inner being craves to taste and feast on a dimension of life not reduced to the fading surface and fragile realities perceived by our senses. We are wired in our make-up to be sustained by the very Thought that conceived us!

For many, their role models have become the fashion-world beauties, movie stars, pop-idols or sport heroes. Somehow we have mastered the thrill of projecting ourselves to shadow-live in the looks or achievement of others. Their win or loss becomes ours! Millions of people are caught up in this fascinating fantasy world. Life has become reduced to a LOTTO. We count the days to the next lucky draw and continue to imagine a million.

We scorn or try to ignore the statistics that embarrass or expose us: prisons have become the garbage heap of our society. We are reluctant to acknowledge that our Correctional Service system fails to rehabilitate the criminal. In 2003 in South Africa more than 85% of released prisoners will return to crime, and back to prisons, which are already 70% overcrowded. Some prisons in SA are almost 300% overcrowded. It costs the taxpayer more than R500 million per month to keep the prisons going. This is almost R3000 per month per criminal, which is more than three times the minimum wage. (At the time of this writing 2002) This figure only reflects direct prison costs, and does not even include the many related costs, such as policing, prosecuting and the constant insurance hikes, which are due to the ever-increasing spiral of crime. Somehow in our efforts to rehabilitate, all the energy is spent on targeting the cobwebs instead of killing the spider. Crime, juvenile delinquency, drug addiction, and alcohol-abuse, the abuse of women and children, the divorce-rate, the breakup of the family, corruption and war make a mockery of our social, religious and political structures.

Heart transformation exceeds behavioural modification.

Nowhere has life become more worthless than in the context of war. Violence as a voice, whether it be a minority such as al-Qaeda or the Boeremag or a majority such as the Bush and Blair-administration, says the same thing: we have a sick society with a sick self-image. To ignore the value of the human spirit is to insult the integrity of our design.

This becomes such a complex thing; we are prepared to spend millions to save life and at the same time we spend millions to destroy life. We have failed in our basic

education when we fail to appreciate or respect life in its multi-faceted context.

Should our mutual respect for one another be challenged, our highest moral value is at risk.

No man can live happily who regards himself alone,
who turns everything to his own advantage.
One must live for another if one wishes to live for oneself.
True fiends are the whole world to one another.
He that is a friend to himself is also a friend to mankind.

Seneca B.C.3 - A.D.65 Rome

FAITH PERCEPTION

In this study I wish to explore and disclose the secret that I believe empowers the individual to live beyond the confines of the frustrating restrictions of a pot-bound, dwarfed existence. It will release you to live beyond disappointment and free you from anxiety, the fear of failure, and the fear of death.

There is a law, which dramatically challenges and cancels the gravity-effect of condemnation, guilt, inferiority and the persistent pull of negative habits.

It is called the law of perfect liberty; the mirror image of your authentic design, captured, preserved and revealed in Christ. James 1:18, 23-25 Mirror Bible

We attach much value to the applause and recognition of our fellow man. Exceptional performance makes you public property. Yet the same crowd who praises you today would more than likely crucify you tomorrow, should the impression of the performance fade, disappoint or fail.

While many only dream of wealth and fame, others hide within the confined space of popular brand names: wear the right clothes, drive a certain kind of car, and be seen with the right crowd etcetera; 'blend' becomes the magic word. Because of the fear of rejection, the individual dare not be different. The feeling of being accepted by the crowd gives one some sense of security and belonging, yet this sought after space becomes the very trap that dwarfs the individual.

Masses barely survive and are forced to live below the breadline, without any realistic thought or chance to ever change or escape the deadly routine. Generations of both the rich and the poor live and die within a bonsai-mindset.

If it were true that man is essentially spirit, then to discover our spirit origin and identity would inevitably release a new dimension of thinking and expression! Your thoughts lead the way to your spirit, the inner core of your being. Here the code of your origin and spirit identity is stored in much the same way in which the cells in your body preserve the DNA code of your genetic identity.

Life is a fragile flame in its human frame, but an eternal blaze in its spirit age. Yet even in its physical shrine of clay, it reveals a tenacity that stubbornly survives and conquers onslaught of time and challenge.

We can trace our lineage and ancestors to ancient mankind, but is it possible to ultimately perceive our origin in God? Are we the mere product of a big bang, time, evolution and eventual physical conception, or do we share an intelligent common origin beyond our history and genealogy?

On the Internet we master global contact with our fellow man, in spite of geographic, political, cultural and even language barriers. Yet we remain sceptical about our ability to spiritually connect with our Maker and encounter meaningful feedback when we knock on his door, or dare we realise that he is in fact doing the knocking?

"I was ready to be found by those who did not seek me; I said, "Here am I, here am I." Is.65:1

In science we often attempt to reason away the existence of God, while the mere fact that we are, as ultimate evidence that he is, is blatantly and deliberately ignored.

We cannot wish the evidence away. We are the evidence.

The tapestry of life begins with a single thread. A single fertilised egg (zygote), the size of a pinhead, contains chemical instructions that would fill more than 500,000 printed pages! The genetic information contained in this "encyclopaedia" determines every potential physical aspect of the developing human from height to hair colour. In time, the fertilised egg divides into the 75 trillion cells that make up the human body, including 12 billion brain cells, with a capacity to form over 120 trillion connections. A.E.Wilder-Smith

A single DNA strand contains 3 billion individual characters! To appreciate the calculation, consider the fact that 1 million seconds equal 12 days and 1 billion seconds equal 32 years! Thus, to count the individual characters in the DNA of just one of your 75 trillion cells at one character per second, will take 96 years!

"I knew you before I formed you in your mother's womb" Jer.1:5.

"You it was who fashioned my inward parts; you knitted me together in my mother's womb. I praise you for you fill me with awe; wonderful you are, and wonderful your works. You know me through and through. My body was no mystery to you when I was formed in secret, woven in the depths of the earth. 'Thy eyes beheld my unformed substance; in thy book were written, every one of them, the days that were formed for me, when as yet there was none of them.' RSV

How mysterious, O God, are your thoughts to me; how vast in number they are. Were I to try counting them, they would be more than the grains of sand; to finish their count my years must equal yours." Ps 139:13-18. REB.

Every time we love, encounter joy or experience beauty, a hint of the nature of our Maker reflects within us; even in the experience of the unbeliever.

Rom.1:19 "...even though God is not a stranger to them, for what can be known of God is already manifest in them. Rom 1:20 God is on display in creation; the very fabric of visible cosmos appeals to reason. It clearly bears witness to the ever present sustaining power and intelligence of the invisible God, leaving man without any valid excuse to ignore him. Rom 1:21 Yet man only knew him in a philosophical religious way from a distance, and failed to give him credit as God. Their taking him for granted and lack of gratitude veiled him from them; they became absorbed in useless debates and discussions which further darkened their understanding about themselves. Rom 1:22 Their wise conclusions only proved folly." Mirror Bible

Our ability to perceive and appreciate value is an extension of our Maker's attributes. "The seeing eye and the hearing ear, the Lord has made them both." Proverbs 20:12.

Our yearning for a sense of total fulfilment and meaning keeps us searching beyond temporal and sensual gratification. If God does exist and if he is indeed the architect of the universe; responsible for the pattern of things and the electrical charge of the atom and the unique individual structure of the molecule, then no one will question the fact that he must be the most awesome and attractive Being in the universe. Then to know and intimately encounter him must be life's greatest gift. To doubt him, is to remain reduced to a philosophy of chance and loneliness. There exists no possible calculation of time that could give chance a fair chance to form just one of the most simple protein molecules, let alone repeat it.

Faith is to our spirit what our senses are to our bodies. Heb 11:6 There is no substitute [1]reward for faith. Faith's return exceeds any other sense of achievement. Faith knows that God is; those who desire to respond to his invitation to draw near, realize by faith that he is life's most perfect gift. *(If he is the desired one then no substitute will suffice. Jesus Christ defines God's faith; he is Emmanuel. He is the substance and evidence of all that God believes. Jesus is what God believes. The word translated "reward" is the word [1]misthapodotes. This word is only used once in the Bible and is an interesting combination of two words, misthoo, a wage and apodidomi to give away; righteousness is revealed by faith as a gift and not as a reward for keeping the law; faith pleases God, not good or bad behavior.)* Mirror. His reward is himself. Genesis 15:1. Man was not designed to live in loneliness and spiritual isolation.

The mystery is within us and in all that lives, even in the bodies of the small

16

fishes in the sea-pools, the mystery of the being of God. There is no creature that breathes but the breathing is the rhythm of his love, no flower that glows with any other light but his, no voice that speaks in kindness but the cadence of the compassion is his own. Elizabeth Goudge.

Psa 24:1 "The earth is the LORD's and the fulness thereof, the world and those who dwell therein." The thief has no ownership rights; he is only the father of lies. "Bring me a coin, whose inscription and image does it bear? Return to Caesar what belongs to him and return to God what belongs to him." Luk 15. You cannot be lost unless you belong! Even in his lost state, mankind remains the property of God. Jesus is God's great invitation to the human race, "Return to your Father; you are his off-spring!" Psa 22:27 "All the ends of the earth shall remember and turn to the LORD; and all the families of the nations shall worship before him."

We are designed for divine encounter. Tangible beyond touch our hearts embrace and echo him. Our most intimate and urgent quest becomes satisfied when we discover our true origin and identity reflected and redeemed in him. Every sense of veil or distance is cancelled. We are spotless and clean! "And we all, with new understanding, see ourselves in him as in a mirror; thus we are changed from an inferior mindset to the revealed opinion of our true likeness and innocence." 2 Cor. 3:18.

As much as the world of science depends upon the senses to perceive, measure and calculate the facts and then to form reliable conclusion, faith perceives the reality of God and extends the evidence to reason. Faith is not wishful thinking; Jesus Christ is the substance of faith; he is both the author and conclusion of faith. He is the accurate measure of the blueprint of our design, the image and likeness of God in human form. Eph.4:7 The gift of Christ gives dimension to grace and defines our individual value. Grace was given to each one of us according to the measure of the gift of Christ.

Anticipate the revelation of Christ within you.

WEIGHING WORDS

Words are spirit vehicles. Whenever a windmill is erected, wind that remained untapped for ages can now be harvested and harnessed into an essential power source.

We have discovered and mastered the technology of transmission and reception. The airwaves are bursting with information, around the clock. It all remains invisible and inaudible until a receiver is tuned to a specific frequency.

The ear is designed to hear the voice of our Maker. "Whoever has an ear to hear let him hear." God's eternal voice has found an expression in the incarnation to be known and read by all men.

The following quotation describes the experience of a little girl listening to her stepfather reading from the Bible: *"All through the Book, even in the dreadful parts, the language would now and then suddenly affect her like an enchantment. The peculiarities of Father Sprigg's delivery worried her not at all. It was as though his gruff voice tossed the words roughly in the air separate particles of no great value, and immediately they fell again transmuted, like the music of a peal of bells or raindrops shot through with sunshine and vista beyond vista of incomparable beauty opened before the mind. It was a mystery to Stella that mere words could make this happen. She supposed the makers of these phrases had fashioned them to hold their visions as one makes a box to hold one's treasure, and Father Sprigg's voice was the key grating in the lock, so that the box could open and set them free. That transmutation in the air still remained as unexplainable as the sudden change in herself, when at the moment of the magical fall her dull mind became suddenly sparkling with wonder and her spirit leaped up inside her like a bird..."* Gentian Hill by Elizabeth Goudge.

A word in any language can be most fascinating. Seed stores the life energy and the genetic detail of a plant species, in much the same way thoughts and concepts are concealed in words and language.

A positive environment is the only contribution seed requires. My Dad always kept a few chickens in our backyard. As children we were often so keen for the hens to become broody so that we could start counting down the days for the eggs to hatch. It fascinated me to watch the broody hen sit on that nest regardless of the weather. She certainly counted her chickens before they were hatched; if she didn't she would never become broody! Faith inspires wisdom of a different kind.

In Acts 14:1 Luke writes that "Paul preached in such a way, that many believed."

Faith is not something we do to get God to do something back to us; faith is what happens to us when we realize what God has already done for us!

I once participated in a vegetable garden project in Zwelihle Township in Hermanus. I learned a simple principle: when the soil is well prepared and the beds are properly dressed and cared for, it is more likely for the seed to produce a hundred-fold. We cannot add to the quality of the seed, the seed trodden under foot or eaten by birds or the seed that produces an abundant harvest were the same seed. No man can duplicate what the seed alone can do. Yet we can do much to the soil in preparing the ideal environment the seed requires. Nothing prepares the soil of faith better than the confident declaring of the completed work of Christ in redeeming the life of our design; revealing to every person how loved they are, how forgiven they are, how included and represented they are in Christ. This is the power ingredient of our prayers and our preaching. "The love of God constrains us, because we are convinced that one has died for all, therefore all have died." 2 Cor.5:14. In the economy of God, what happened to Christ happened to mankind, before anyone but God believed it.

The Gospel according to Mathew, Mark, Luke and John all record how Jesus proclaimed good news, taught its dynamic implication and then healed many people. Math 4:23,24; Math 9:35. His preaching and teaching awakened faith in the minds and hearts of the people. He often referred to the faith response of the audience: "Let it be to you according to your faith!" His life and teaching declared his Father's desire and persuasion to heal the broken heart and set the captives free. He spoke of great faith and little faith and always responded to visible faith; "...when he saw their faith..."

By design human life is wired to believe. We are faith creatures in our make-up; we want to believe. Love realized awakens belief. When you know that you are loved, it is easy to believe. Love sets faith in motion. Gal 5:6

Faith creates the environment for divine encounter. You are the god-kind by design and therefore you are faith compatible. Faith is the key; this kind of faith has its exclusive origin in God's persuasion about you.

Jesus is God's mind made up about you. Jesus is what God believes about you. Our faith does not persuade God; his faith persuades us!

Faith comes to you in the revelation of what God has done on your behalf in Christ. Romans 10:17 "It is clear then that faith's [1]source is found in the content of the message heard; the message is Christ." (We are God's

19

audience; Jesus is God's language! The Greek, [1]ek, is a preposition that denotes source or origin; thus, faith comes out of the word that reveals Christ.) Rom 1:17 "Herein lies the secret of the power of the Gospel; there is no good news in it until the [1]righteousness of God is revealed! The dynamic of the gospel is the revelation of God's faith as the only valid basis for our belief. The prophets wrote in advance about the fact that God believes that righteousness unveils the life that he always had in mind for us. "Righteousness by his (God's) faith defines life." *(The good news is the fact that the Cross of Christ was a success. God rescued [1]the life of our design; he redeemed our [1]innocence. Man would never again be judged righteous or unrighteous by his own ability to obey moral laws! It is not about what man must or must not do but about what Jesus has done! It is from faith to faith, and not man's good or bad behavior or circumstances interpreted as a blessing or a curse [Hab 2:4]. Instead of reading the curse when disaster strikes, Habakkuk realizes that the Promise out-dates performance as the basis to man's acquittal. Deuteronomy 28 would no longer be the motivation or the measure of right or wrong behavior! "Though the fig trees do not blossom, nor fruit be on the vines, the produce of the olive fail and the fields yield no food, the flock be cut off from the fold and there be no herd in the stalls, yet I will rejoice in the Lord, I will joy in the God of my salvation. God, the Lord, is my strength; he makes my feet like hinds' feet, he makes me tread upon my high places [Hab 3:17-19 RSV]. "Look away [from the law of works] unto Jesus; he is the Author and finisher of faith." [Heb 12:1]. The gospel is the revelation of the righteousness of God; it declares how God succeeded to put mankind right with him. It is about what God did right, not what Adam did wrong. The word righteousness comes from the Anglo Saxon word, "rightwiseness;" wise in that which is right. In Greek the root word for righteousness is [1]dike, which means two parties finding likeness in each other. The Hebrew word for righteousness is [1]tzadok, which refers to the beam in a scale of balances. In Colossians 2:9-10, It is in Christ that God finds an accurate and complete expression of himself, in a human body! He mirrors our completeness and is the ultimate authority of our true identity.)*

God's faith in you, rubs off on you! "Paul preached in such a way that many believed." Acts 14:1. He proclaimed the completed work of Christ on the cross in such a way that there would be no ground for doubt or compromise. The Dodrich translation reads, "the model of doctrine instructs you as in a mould." Romans 6:17. Now at Lystra there was a man who was a cripple from birth. He listened to Paul speaking; and Paul, looking intently at him, and seeing that he had faith to be made well, said in a loud voice: "Stand upright on your feet!" He jumped up and walked for the first time in his life. Acts 14:9-11. Imagine this dear man's mindset; embarrassed and embittered; now suddenly he hears a message that turns on the light of life in his understanding; he sees himself mirrored in Paul's message; mirrored in the sacrificed Lamb by whose stripes his healing was redeemed!

Your belief in God does not define him; his faith in what he knows to be true about you defines you.

In Mark 11:22 Jesus says, "have the faith of God." Unfortunately most translations say, "have faith in God"; there is a vast difference. God's belief in you gives substance to your faith. The good news reveals God's faith in man. It reveals how God succeeded to rescue his image in man.

Your faith reflects God's opinion of you. Your faith reveals the value you place upon God's faith in you. "The life that I now live in the flesh I live by the faith of the Son of God." Gal. 2:20. (Greek text, "the faith of" not "faith in")

One of the saddest scriptures in the Bible is in Hebrews 4:2, "The word which they heard did not benefit them, because it did not mix together with faith." God does not force or impose himself on man. He implores man with his love, but would never threaten man into making a decision. A relationship has no virtue outside of mutual consent. The most foolish thing about man is the fact that he has the ability to harden his heart and resist or even delay the blessing and purpose of God in his life!

Heb 8:9 This time we will be making a new agreement, completely unlike the previous one based on external ritual. I had literally to take your hand and lead you out of slavery from Egypt, yet you refused to spontaneously follow or trust in me; I could never abide your indifference. *(God prophesies a covenant that will not be subject to the same defect of the previous one; one that was spoon fed to Israel and whose obligations they yet failed to meet. God had to take them by the hand to lead them out of Egypt. This time, he promised, I will put my laws into their minds and write them it upon their hearts.)*

Heb 8:10 Now, instead of documenting my laws on stone, I will chisel them into your mind and engrave them in your inner consciousness; it will no longer be a one-sided affair. I will be your God and you will be my people, not by compulsion but by mutual desire.

Heb 4:1 What a foolish thing it would be for us if we should now fail in a similar fashion to enter into the full consequences of our redemption.

Heb 4:2 The gospel we have heard today is the same gospel that was preached in the promise. *(Both share the same source, intent and content, although the first was a mere shadow of the second).* God had mankind in mind all along, yet, because people lacked the persuasion by which the word could be ignited and brought to life in them, the promise did not profit them at all.

Heb 4:3 Faith *(not our own works)* secures our entrance into God's rest *(into the result of his completed work).* Hear the echo of God's cry though the ages,

"Oh! If only they would enter into my rest." His rest celebrates perfection. The sufficiency of his rest is founded upon the fact that his work is complete; even the fall of humanity did not flaw its perfection. *(His rest was not at risk. "His works were finished from the foundation of the world". "My wrath" orge, passionate desire, any strong outburst of emotion, "Oh! If only they would enter into my rest." First Adam failed to enter into God's finished work, and then Israel failed to enter into the consequence of their complete redemption out of Egypt and as a result of their unbelief perished in the wilderness. Now let us not fail in the same manner to see the completed work of the cross. How God desires for us to see the same perfection; what he saw when he first created man in his image and then again what he saw in the perfect obedience of his Son when he was wounded for our transgressions. Because of the cross he succeeded to perfectly redeem and restore human life to likeness and innocence.*

God is not in his rest because he is exhausted, but because he is satisfied with what he sees and knows concerning us! He now invites us with urgent persuasion to enter into what he sees.

"From the foundation of the world." apo, away from, before, kataballo, cast down, sometimes translated foundation, see notes on Eph. 1:4 "This association goes back to before the fall of the world, his love knew that he would present us again face to face before him, identified in Christ in blameless innocence."

The implications of the fall are completely cancelled out. kataballo - "to fall away, to put in a lower place," instead of themelios - "foundation" see Eph.2:20 - Thus translated "the fall of the world" instead of "the foundation of the world.")

Heb 4:4 Scripture records the seventh day to be the prophetic celebration of God's perfect work. What God saw satisfied his scrutiny. *(Behold, it is very good, and God rested from all his work. Gen.1:31, 2:2; God saw more than his perfect image in Adam, he also saw the Lamb and his perfect work of redemption! "The Lamb having been slain from the foundation of the world." Rev.13:8. "That which has been is now; that which is to be, already has been;" Ecc 3:15)*

Heb 4:5 In Psalm 95 the same seventh day metaphor is reiterated: "O, that they would enter my rest!"

Today when you hear his voice, I pray that the eyes of your understanding will be enlightened to discover the full measure of God's completed work in Christ, in you!

We do not need to conjure up our own faith when we can be persuaded about what God believes. Jesus is what God believes about you; he mirrors the life of your design redeemed in his death and resurrection.

Nothing we do can get God to love us more!

We are of flawless design, and have a flawless redemption, and we are called into a flawless fellowship, forever! If this was not true, the gospel would be a mere fairy tale.

THE LAW OF SPONTANEITY

To act right simply because it is ones duty is proper;
but a good action which is the result of no law of obligation
shines more than any. Thomas Hardy.

In the New Testament, James, the younger brother of Jesus, writes about a dynamic concept, which he calls 'the law of perfect liberty'. James 1:17,18,23-25. This law dramatically challenges the way we think and feel about ourselves. James speaks about the word of truth that reflects the face of man's birth (genesis) as in a mirror. He calls this word, which proclaims God as our true origin, the law of perfect liberty. To perceive God as our origin and to discover in Christ how perfectly God succeeded to redeem his image in human form, ignites a new order and quality of spontaneous life. The law of perfect liberty in the Greek, nomon teleion eleutherias, means the following: nomon, law, order, teleios, complete or perfect, eleutherias, unrestrained, exempt from obligation or liability, spontaneous. (Inspired by faith and not by willpower).

Religion traditionally proclaims and promotes man's responsibility and obligation to observe strict prescribed codes of conduct. Only within the implicit obedience of these could man wish to score some points. The more we struggled to do the right thing the greater the sense of condemnation and guilt became whenever we failed. To even imagine a life without obligation and exempt from liability sounds reckless and irresponsible. Surely this law of spontaneity can be nothing more than wishful thinking. Yet the effect of this law guarantees a life expression of total fulfilment and liberty, complete, perfect and lacking in nothing. James 1:4. We all know that the experience in 'real' life is often in sharp contrast. We have accepted the fact that we are incomplete, imperfect and will always be in lack.

Could it be possible for the average man on the street to know such a life of total bliss, or is this exclusively reserved for those who qualify as "super spooky-spiritual"?

The law of perfect liberty does not rely on man's ability and disciplined performance to obey and perform routine regulations and commandments. Like the law of gravity, this law works spontaneously within a specific 'magnetic' field of influence. Living under the law of Moses or any moral law for that matter, depends entirely upon the individual's willpower and self-discipline to consistently adhere to and obey the requirements of the law. Thus the law of obligation became the basis of man's experience of condemnation, and a sense of failure and shortcoming. What keeps religion enslaved to this law is fear of punishment and a hope for reward, whether it is the thought of escaping hell and gaining heaven one day, or at least the pious feeling of applause and recognition now. Any measure of success achieved produced a 'holier than thou' attitude, which could easily become the breeding ground for hypocrisy.

The need to be noticed and applauded became more important to the Pharisees than the good deed in itself. Mathew 6:1-8.

Under the law of obligation, doing remains a duty and not a spontaneous lifestyle. So much of religious zeal and energy involves man's endeavour and effort to do things that will hopefully qualify him to be accepted by God. But sadly, within the day-to-day experience of most, the sense of distance between the Creator and the creature seems to prevail. Ultimately, man remains isolated through feelings of guilt, inferiority and disappointment, and is left with a vague hope that God will feel sorry enough for his pathetic and miserable creatures to eventually excuse them and still slip them into his heaven one day in the sweet by and by. That is, if there is a God after all. The less spiritual feedback we encounter, the more we become dependent upon programs and structures of religious routine and rituals to at least keep the process going in the absence of God. It does not really matter what we believe, as long as we just believe, we imagine.

God is so much bigger than religious or philosophical debates about him; as much as experiencing him is bigger than religion's most eloquent definition of him.

Someone once said: "A man with an encounter is not at the mercy of a man with an argument."

When one falls in love, one experiences a glimpse of the law of spontaneity: suddenly you cannot do enough to please your partner; no sacrifice is too great, everything is shared in the most unselfish manner. You look at the other person with eyes which are new. Maybe you even grew up together but never really noticed each other; yet, now you cannot get the person out of your mind. You are thrilled with delight at the mere thought to be in the company and arms of the one you love. Life takes on a brand-new meaning. You find yourself to be more tolerant even with people around you who would previously irritate you and drive you crazy. Your total attitude and outlook on life is renewed. Life is bliss.

They say no one is perfect until you fall in love.

Sadly though, the goose bumps seem to gradually disappear and we accept the fact that maybe life was never meant to always be such a high-peak experience.

We were just beginning to soar into a new dimension when we came back to earth with a thud. Maybe life is only a marathon and struggle where a select few survive to the bitter end?

In Christ God is not teasing us with possibilities beyond our reach; he gives definition to the life of our design, our authentic and original value as in a mirror. This is our constant; our rock reference; our foundation that remains the same in any size storm or contradiction.

Here are the four most common influences that motivate behaviour:

- Fear of failure or punishment.

- The attraction of reward or recognition.

- The force of habit or addiction.

- Spontaneous life, inspired by love.

You can get a person to do almost anything if you can starve or scare him enough or promise him a big enough reward. The law of works is driven by willpower; the law of faith is inspired by love. Rom 3:27 The law of faith cancels the law of works; which means there is suddenly nothing left for man to boast in. No one is superior to another. *(Bragging only makes sense if there is someone to compete with or impress. "While we compete with one another and compare ourselves with one another we are without understanding. [2 Cor 10:12]. "Through the righteousness of God we have received a faith of equal standing." [See 2 Pet 1:1 RSV] The OS (operating system) of the law of works is willpower; the OS of the law of faith is love. Gal 5:6 Love sets faith in motion.)*

A man was carrying a very ill person over a long distance when someone asked him if the load he carried was not too heavy for him. "He ain't heavy, he's my brother," came the prompt reply. This man's attitude is the theme of the law of liberty. The law of love liberates one into a different level of life. Its language is not "have to" but "want to". There is a distinct difference between willpower and willingness. This law governs the will of man, not through a sense of obligation but inspiration and passion, with a love that desires to please.

Faith-inspiration is the purest energy of the soul. This level of inspiration is fuelled not by reasoning or emotion, but by a revelation of worth. God's faith in you declares your value; realized value ignites appreciation. Make it a habit to appreciate one another beyond performance or disappointment. When true value is realized it becomes so easy to admire.

To hear the word of truth of your original design and redeemed identity is to see the face of your birth as in a mirror. You cannot fault that image, or flaw the likeness; even at close scrutiny every detail of your original design remains intact and confirms that you are complete and perfect and without lack. This is the fuel of faith that produces a joy that overcomes all contradiction. James 1:2-4,17,18,23-25.

To believe that God is, and that he is indeed the origin of your being, sets the stage to experience him. The face-to-face encounter with the mirror reflection of your true and redeemed origin, preserved and perceived in Jesus, the blueprint of God's thought, ignites the law of perfect liberty. Just like when "the ugly duckling" suddenly realized in the reflection of its image the truth that freed the swan to be swan indeed, Jesus is not merely an example for us but of us!

"A work of art is like a human being, the more it is admired the more beautiful it grows, reflecting the gift of love like light back to the giver" Elizabeth Goudge.

In your every relationship begin to discover and declare the value of the other. Your reference is Christ and his completed work. He is your constant! In him we no longer know anyone from a human point of view! 2 Cor.5:14,16, Acts 10:28, Titus 3:2-4.

God desires closeness, not distance. You are designed to live a totally fulfilled life.

One of our most basic human rights is to feel appreciated. We long for recognition. Nothing harms a relationship or self image more than to feel neglected or taken for granted. Love and friendship blossom in an environment of appreciation. It is in the nature of love to admire without prejudice.

Yet, love can afford to be misunderstood, ignored, face conflict, injustice and war, and still conquer.

To appreciate means to express and communicate value. But value must have a realized, realistic reference, a reference that goes beyond our best, or poorest performance.

Why would God go to the extremes that he did to persuade sinful mankind of his love for them? Did God merely send Jesus out of pity for the human race? His love is certainly not a reward for good behavior!

Salvation reveals a calculation that God made to redeem his image and likeness in human form!

In Mat 13:44 "The kingdom of heaven is like treasure hidden in a field, which a man found and covered up; then in his joy he goes and sells all that he has and buys that field.

Romans 5:6 God's timing was absolutely perfect; humanity was at their weakest when Christ died their death. *(We were bankrupt in our efforts to save ourselves.)*

Rom 5:7 It is most unlikely that someone will die for another man, even if he is righteous; yet it is remotely possible that someone can brave such devotion that he would actually lay down his own life in an effort to save the life of an extraordinary good person.

Rom 5:8 Herein is the extremity of God's love gift: mankind was rotten to the core when Christ died their death.

Rom 5:9 If God could love us that much when we were ungodly and guilty, how much more are we free to realize his love now that we are declared innocent by his blood? *(God does not love us more now that we are reconciled to him; we are now free to realize how much he loved us all along! [Col 2:14, Rom 4:25])*

Rom 5:10 Our hostility and indifference towards God did not reduce his love for us; he saw equal value in us when he exchanged the life of his son for ours. Now that the act of [1]reconciliation is complete, his life in us saves us from the gutter-most to the uttermost. *(Reconciliation, from [1]katalasso, meaning a mutual exchange of equal value. To exchange, as coins for others of equivalent value. "For if while we were enemies we were reconciled to God by the death of his Son, much more, now that we are reconciled, shall we be saved by his life." — RSV)*

Rom 5:11 Thus, our joyful boasting in God continues; Jesus Christ has made reconciliation a reality.

My passion and mission in life is to help ordinary people realise the integrity of their authentic individual value and escape the frustrating routine and ritual of a mere bonsai existence.

Nothing is more rewarding than to discover the real person in another person. Only discovering the real person in yourself equals that. We are fashioned in the same mould, the expression of the same thought. Our author's signature and invisible image is nowhere better preserved or displayed than in our inner consciousness. Our origin traces the very imagination of God.

Man began in God.

We are not the invention of our parents. It is not our brief history on planet earth that introduces us to God; he knew us before he formed us in our mother's womb! Jer 1:5.

Every human life is equally valued and represented in Christ. He gives context and reference to our being as in a mirror; not as an example for us, but of us. The "ugly duckling" saw reflected in the water the truth that freed the swan! Ps 23 says, "He leads me beside still waters, and restores my soul" or this can be translated, "by the waters of reflection my soul remembers who I am!"

You are the expression of the greatest idea that ever was! God imagined you!

Every invention begins with an original thought. You are God's original thought. You are his initiative; the result of his creative inspiration, his intimate design and love-dream. The first Hebrew word in the Bible, *berosh*, literally means "in the head". No wonder then that God is mindful of you! You are his work of art; his poem says Paul in the Greek text of Eph.2:10.

He redeemed your life from destruction, not with perishable currency, but with the priceless blood of Jesus.

Awake to his image within you! In the same way as seed conceives within the womb, he reveals himself within your being. The moment an idea ignites, it creates its own space, momentum and destiny.

During the years of depression a preacher told the story of the talents to his congregation, and after the message gave each one present half a crown. One of the ladies immediately went and bought some flour and proceeded to bake rusks under the most difficult circumstances and in the smallest of kitchens. Few people today realise that the Ouma Rusks and Simba Chips they buy in every Supermarket and Café in South Africa, were lying hidden within that first half a crown.

The gospel revealed in an awakened life is an open letter, "a living epistle" known and read by all men; it appeals to every man's conscience. 2 Cor 3:2, 4:2.

(The Latin word conscience means a joint seeing; also the Greek word for conscience, *suneido* means, to see together.)

Lying dormant in the heart of every human is a consciousness of the likeness and image of God, capsuled in the incorruptible seed. At the core of our being we all share likeness with God and with one another.

To realize the image of God in everyone is to discover our common blueprint.

On the surface, every human seems very different from the next. But when you get down to the nitty gritty of our genetics, the most that any two people might differ from each other is a mere one hundredth of one percent. Only 0.01 percent of our genes is reflected in our external appearance, whatever our racial or historic background is.

We share so much common ground that we actually have 99,9% reason to be every one's friend! The common ground humanity shares in Christ makes friendship 100% possible. To discover this will make divorce and war impossible!

2 Cor 10:12 Not that we venture to class or compare ourselves with some of those who commend themselves. But when they measure themselves by one another, and compare themselves with one another, they are without understanding. Rsv.

The fact that we are different gives us distinct value. Each of us can make an individual, authentic contribution to life that no one can repeat or compete with!

Life finds unique expression in you, beyond your fingerprint. You are indeed irreplaceable!

Herein lies the genius of God; he values each one of us individually.

This explains the cross: Why would God bother to go to such length to rescue corrupt and hostile mankind? Market value is established only by the price someone is prepared to pay. The virtue of such love cannot be accredited to the mere sorry state of the human race or the pity of the Creator. God saw enough calculated value in every person to justify the price he paid for humanity's redemption from sin, guilt and fear. He successfully redeemed his image and likeness in us. "The kingdom of heaven is like a treasure hidden in an agricultural field, which a man discovered and covered up; then in his joy he goes and sells all that he has and buys that field." Mathew 13:44. Paul reveals in 1 Corinthians 2:7,8, why this treasure was covered up. (See the chapter on "The Mystery revealed.")

Through the sacrificial death of Jesus Christ, God vindicated man beyond anything that could ever disqualify or condemn him. The Lamb of God took away the sins of the world. "Our sins resulted in his death; his resurrection is proof of our acquittal." Rom.4:25. This is one of the most important statements in the entire Bible. Why was Jesus handed over to die? Because of our sins. Why was he raised from the dead? Because we were justified! His resurrection reveals our righteousness! (Notice in both sentences the Greek word, dia, because of, is used.)

If man was still guilty after Jesus died, his resurrection would neither be possible nor relevant! This explains Acts 10:28 and 2 Cor.5:14,16.

Adam's transgression no longer holds the human race hostage. Rom 5:7,8,12-21

Many theologians are quick to believe in the global impact of Adam's fall, but fail to credit the cross with a far greater significance, out of all proportion to Adam's sin. The same humanity that stood condemned in Adam now stands justified and forgiven in Christ! Rom.5:18,19.

God believes in you, whether you believe in him or not.

The lost coin never lost its original identity or value. Being lost simply kept it out of circulation. "Suppose a woman has 10 silver coins and loses one. Does she not light a lamp, sweep the house and search diligently until she finds it." Luke 15:8-10. In His next breath, Jesus tells the parable of the lost son. One night God revealed to me the tear-stained face of my mother in a dream. She was on her knees, sweeping the house in search for her lost coin! I thank God for praying mothers!

"Bring me a coin, whose image and inscription does it bear?" Luke 20:20-26. He might as well have said, "Bring me a man, whose image and inscription does he bear?" The image and inscription of God is engraved in our inner consciousness. "Return to Caesar what belongs to him, and to God what is his."

By reminding yourself or someone else of shortcoming and failure, you are veiling the liberating truth of the life of your design mirrorred and redeemed in Christ.

Rom 8:1 Now the decisive conclusion is this: in Christ, every bit of condemning evidence against us is cancelled. *("Who walk not after the flesh but after the spirit" This sentence was not in the original text, but later copied from verse 4. The person who added this most probably felt that the fact of Paul's declaration of mankind's innocence had to be made subject again to man's conduct. Religion under the law felt more comfortable with the condition of personal contribution rather than the conclusion of what faith reveals. The "in Christ" revelation is key to God's dealing with man. It is the PIN-code of the Bible. See 1Cor 1:30 and Eph 1:4.)*

Rom 8:2 The law of the Spirit is the liberating force of life in Christ. This leaves us with no further obligation to the law of sin and death. Spirit has superseded the sin enslaved senses as the principle law of our lives. *(The law of the spirit is righteousness by faith vs the law of personal effort and self righteousness which produces condemnation and spiritual death which is the fruit of the DIY tree.)*

Rom 8:3 The law failed to be anything more than an instruction manual; it had no power to deliver mankind from the strong influence of sin holding us hostage in our own bodies. God disguised himself in his son in this very domain where sin ruled man, the human body. The flesh body he lived and conquered in was no different to ours. Thus sin's authority in the human body was condemned. *(Heb 4:15 As High Priest he fully identifies with us in the context of our frail human life. Having subjected it to close scrutiny, he proved that the human frame was master over sin. His sympathy with us is not to be seen as excusing weaknesses that are the result of a faulty design, but rather as a trophy to humanity. He is not an example for us but of us.)*

Rom 8:4 The righteousness promoted by the law is now realized in us. Our practical day-to-day-life bears witness to spirit inspiration and not flesh domination.

Rom 8:5 Sin's symptoms are sponsored by the senses, a mind dominated by the sensual. Thoughts betray source; spirit life attracts spirit thoughts.

Rom 8:6 Thinking patterns are formed by reference, either the sensual appetites of the flesh and spiritual death, or zoe-life and total tranquillity flowing from a mind addicted to spirit (faith) realities.

LOVE DISPELS FEAR

Your life can be inspired by love or ruled by fear. Fear is not a force in itself; it is merely the unawareness of love. Darkness is not a force; it is the absence of light. We give experiences, circumstances, rumors or people power over us by the way we perceive and respond to them.

In 2 Cor 4:4 Paul says that unbelief empowers the defeated god of this world to blindfold us in order to keep us from seeing the light of the gospel. The light of the gospel reveals the glory of God in the face of the man Jesus Christ who is the image of God, AS IN A MIRROR!

2Cor 4:3 If our message seems vague to anyone, it is not because we are withholding something from certain people! It is just because some are so stubborn in their efforts to uphold an outdated system, that they don't see it! They are all equally found in Christ but they prefer to remain lost in the cul-de-sac language of the law! 2 Cor 4:4 The survival- and self improvement programs of the [1]religious systems of this world veil the minds of the unbelievers; exploiting their ignorance about their true origin and their redeemed innocence. The veil of unbelief obstructs a person's view and keeps one from seeing what the light of the gospel so clearly reveals: the [2]glory of God is the image and likeness of our Maker redeemed in human form; this is what the gospel of Christ is all about. *(The god of this [1]aion, age, refers to the religious systems and governing structures of this world. The unbelief that neutralized Israel in the wilderness was the lie that they believed about themselves; "We are grasshoppers, and the 'enemy' is a giant towering over us!" Num 13:33, Josh 2:11, Heb 4:6, "They failed to possess the promise due to unbelief." The blueprint [2]doxa, glory of God is what Adam lost on humanity's behalf. See Eph 4:18)*

Herein is love perfected, in that we know and believe the love that God has for us. 1 John 4:16-19. Perfect love dispels fear.

Love fuels faith. Gal 5:6.

Irritation, sarcasm, suspicion, anger, and self-pity are snares that will neutralize you. Whatever happened in your life to cause anger, resentment, self-pity or regret, is now past tense and history; to continue to harbor these thoughts within you, keeps the poison in your system. Forgiveness based upon our true original value redeemed in Christ, releases the flow and healing virtue of the love of God. Titus 3:2-5.

Faith speaks the truth about you.

Faith only communicates what love inspires.

Instead of blame, bless, instead of complain, praise.

Even the biggest failure feels encouraged and challenged rather than intimidated or condemned in the presence of faith.

Jesus was known to be the friend of sinners. No one ever felt condemned or judged unworthy by him. He only judged religious hypocrisy and unbelief.

Faith's reference is the finished work of Christ.Therefore faith forgives; forgiveness sees beyond pain or disappointment.

Fuelled by love, forgiveness cancels the past, sees the future and changes the present. Forgiveness prefers what faith knows.

See man's innocence revealed in Christ, and then it becomes so natural and easy to forgive. "Father, forgive them for they know not what they do!"

Instead of bringing any relief, regret and blame only prolongs the pain.

Faith in the finished work of Christ defeats disappointment.

"We have the same spirit of faith as he had who wrote, "I believe, and so I speak." We too believe and so we speak." 2 Cor.4:13. Here Paul quotes Psalm 116 where David encouraged himself in the Lord, he speaks to himself saying, "Return to your rest O my soul, for the Lord has dealt bountifully with you. I believe and so I speak." Let faith speak. Faith inspiration maintains one exclusive opinion and spontaneously communicates gratitude, appreciation, affection and value.

You can only live one of two lives: a frustrated one or a fulfilled one! Your reference makes the difference! Fulfillment begins with appreciation. Occupy your mind with gratitude instead of criticism and regret. Christ unveiled in you is the ultimate unchallenged reference to gratitude.

The fruit of gratitude is contentment and joy; this takes you beyond resentment, envy, competition or contradiction. Contentment based upon the awareness of who you really are places you beyond threat. Competition, temptation and disappointment will not distract or confuse you. Cultivate an attitude of gratitude.

Today is your gift; every moment is to be celebrated, gratitude is the fuel of joy.

"Gratitude unlocks the fullness of life; it can turn a meal into a feast, a house into a home, a stranger into a friend." Melody Beath.

"To the hungry everything bitter is sweet, but he who is satisfied loathes the honey." Proverbs 27:7.

Nothing makes you more vulnerable than to be driven by a sense of need or lack. Nothing makes you more beautiful than a sense of total fulfilment. The awareness of who we really are and considering the greatness that dwells in us is out of all proportion to the lie of lack and need.

The oldest book in the Bible records the story of Job: here was an extremely devout and wealthy man, trapped in fear. He gives the reason for his fall: "For the thing that I fear comes upon me, and what I dread befalls me." Job 3:25

Job's mind became so cluttered and occupied with fear that he lost sight of who he was and what he had. His fear became the magnetic field that attracted disaster. In fact fear made Job lose his possessions long before he actually lost them. James 1:24.

Fear's focus feeds on frustration, lack, lies, need, worry, anxiety, jealousy, anger, inferiority, suspicion, guilt, depression, ungratefulness, cynicism etc.

Love believes because love knows. Love values truth above performance or disappointment. Jesus embodies the truth about you; he is not an example for you, but of you!

As long as you can find someone or something to blame, you remain trapped.

In blaming someone or something the depressed finds an excuse to remain de-pressed. You are freed the moment you realize that no one can take your quality of life away from you, if no one can stop you from thinking thoughts that truth inspires. Paul explains that we are empowered to arrest every thought to be subject to the consequence of the obedience of Christ. 2 Cor.10:5, Rom.5:19. If you can safeguard your PC with an anti virus program, how much more effective can you guard your heart. We are councelled to guard our hearts more than anything that needs to be guarded; for from it flow the issues of life. Life's every expression finds its source within you.

It is our ignorance of God's faith in us and our unbelief in his love for us that empowers deception. "Perfect love casts out fear; herein is love perfected, in knowing and believing the love that God has for us." 1 John 4:17. "If you continue in my word, you will know the truth, and the truth (about who you are in me) will set you free; whom the Son sets free is free indeed." Remembering our true sonship sets us free! John 8:31-36. There is only one true Father of the human race. "You were unmindful of the Rock that begot you, and you forgot the God who gave you birth." Deut 32:18.

Grasp and believe the truth about yourself, about how complete and free you already are because of Christ, and you will realize that everything you could ever need to make you happy is already within you. "We have this treasure in earthen vessels." 2 Cor 4:7. No amount of sincere prayer could add to the mineral wealth that is already deposited in the earth; all is in place, waiting to be discovered and explored. Col 1:27 In us God desires to exhibit the priceless treasure of Christ's indwelling; every nation will recognize him as in a mirror! The unveiling of Christ in human life completes man's every expectation. *(He is not hiding in history, or in outer space nor in the future, neither in the pages of scripture, he is merely mirrored there to be unveiled within you. Mt 13:44, Gal 1:15, 16)*

Life is not about what you do, it is about who you are. Your career, job-description or achievement can never give you a greater sense of worth and contentment than the simple awareness of who you are, mirrored in Christ. Nothing you could wish to have or achieve or become, can define you more accurately or add more value to your life.

To know who you really are is the essence of all virtue. Everything God designed you for is within you and within your immediate reach.

In John 4 Jesus tells his followers that, by saying "there are yet four months, then comes the harvest" they were looking at the wrong harvest; the fruit of their own labor would never satisfy them! He urges them to look away from that which occupied their expectation and conversation before and to see a harvest that is already ripe! The seed in the ear already matches the seed that was sown! By design man cannot be satisfied by bread alone. The bread of his own labor would disappoint. To feast on the sustenance of spirit union is the true bread; the face to face bread is a celebration of oneness revealed and redeemed in the incarnation!

What God knows to be true about you, exceeds your highest ambition for yourself. What we already are in Christ surpasses anything we could ever wish to become! You are God's dream come true! There is no possible contradiction you could ever face that has what it takes to defeat you!

Many years ago my father bought a Land Rover. On his first off-road trip he got the Landy horribly stuck in the mud. We struggled in vain to get the vehicle out. Mercifully a stranger stopped by to offer his help. Looking into the cabin, he immediately noticed that the 4x4 gear lever was not properly engaged! In a moment the vehicle was out. It was a huge embarrassment, but an even bigger lesson and relief. An off road-vehicle is designed in the first place to handle rough terrain, how much more a human being! Life is meant to be a most exciting adventure. Because of our ignorance of who we are in Christ and him in us we often get stuck in circumstances and struggles where we again try and fight a warfare that has already been won. Become acquainted with Throne room realities, engage your thoughts there; relocate yourself mentally. Col 3:1-3 Mirror Bible.

No one can upset, discredit or humiliate you without your permission.

God has placed a value on your life that is beyond dispute; your true value is a non-negotiable. To forget what manner of man you are, whenever you encounter contradiction, is to deceive yourself. No one can do you greater harm. You are spirit. In essence your spirit is not subject to change. Yet your mind, your mood, your body and your circumstances can all change. You are infinite.

In the 1890's, Marie Curie discovered Radium with an instrument that her husband, Professor Pierre Curie designed. Without this instrument it was impossible to detect its presence. Radium spontaneously and continuously transmits radioactive energy. This valuable and rare element is a mere one millionth of a percent present in the ore that carries it. Yet the ore takes its value from the treasure it holds. This is exactly true about human life. We have this treasure in an earthen vessel. 2 Cor 4:7

Even in the most corrupt and evil life, we must believe that the value of the human spirit remains intact in its full capacity to respond to and reveal the Divine nature. Temperature cannot be measured by a ruler! There is only one valid measure whereby human life is defined: the blueprint of our design. This is what Jesus redeemed. Grace has no greater context! "The gift of Christ gives dimension to grace and defines our individual value." (Grace was given to each one of us according to the measure of the gift of Christ) Eph 4:7.

Something happened to mankind when Jesus died and was raised. The Lamb of God took away the sins of the world! Therefore God says, "call no man unholy or unclean." Acts 10:28.

The full measure of everything God has in mind for man indwells Christ. Col 1:19. And in Chapter 2:10 Paul declares, "We are complete in him!"

"While we compare ourselves with one another and compete with one another, we are without understanding." 2 Cor 10:12.

The lost coin never lost its original value, nor did it change ownership! Luk 15:9, and Luk 20:20-26. You cannot be lost unless you belong!

The discovery of the wealth of our original design redeemed in Christ is life trans-forming. It is like discovering gold in a wasteland! The gold re-defines the original value of the land.

Faith knows the truth about you; faith is to agree with God about you. Because faith knows the truth about someone, faith anticipates and encourages positive change, with patience. Faith ignites the energy for change and growth. God's faith in the finished work of Christ awakens faith in us to no longer tolerate anything in our minds, moods, bodies or circumstances that is inconsistent with our original design. Even old habits are challenged. Negative, genetically transmitted traits lose their hold. Faith creates the environment for radical and permanent change.

The broody hen would stubbornly maintain an uninterrupted temperature around her eggs, regardless of challenging and changing weather conditions or any contradiction to what her instinct (faith) knows. She continues to see the reward. She counts the chickens before they are hatched. It would be wrong to say that she cannot wait for them to hatch; of course she can. She knows! She protects her nest with her life. The wisdom of the world says, "Don't count your chickens before they are hatched!" The wisdom from above says, "If you don't count them before they are hatched, you'll never get broody!"

Faith is not blind, neither is it unconscious; faith knows.

James 1:2 Temptations come in different shapes, sizes and intervals, their intention is always to suck you into their energy field. However my brothers, your joy leads you out triumphantly every time. 1:3 Here is the secret: joy is not something you have to fake, it is the fruit of what your faith knows to be true about you! Knowing that the proof of your faith results in persuasion that remains constant in contradiction. 1:4 (Just like a mother hen patiently broods over her eggs,) steadfastness provides you with a consistent environment, and so patience prevails and proves your perfection; how entirely whole you are and without any shortfall.

"Guard your heart more than anything that needs to be guarded, for from it flow the issues of life." Proverbs 4: 23. Appreciate the content of your heart above all value. In Christ God restored every positive virtue of life to be your true portion. He granted to you everything it takes to live life to the full. Your heart holds the secret to the genesis and authentic blueprint of your life, like the watermark in paper money.

Anticipate a life influenced by the values of your heart. The heart holds out the treasures of life to the hands of thought and words as an apple tree holds out its fruit to the hungry.

The thoughts you think activate the energy fields that dictate the outcome of your day-to-day experience. With Christ as your reference you are free to cultivate a thought pattern that pictures the ultimate life.

38

"A man's life will be of the character of his thoughts" John G Lake.

"It is the habitual thought that frames itself into our lives that affects us even more than our intimate social relations do. Our confidential friends have not so much to do in the shaping of our lives as the thoughts which we harbour." Teale.

A value-conscious focus will continue to block out of your life and mind those distractions, which could possibly hinder you in your embrace of life's excellence. Your thoughts are your sanctuary; your sacred space, your secret place. Love your thoughts!

Our thoughts are silent words that only God and we hear, but those words affect our inner man, our health, our joy and our total attitude. (Unknown)

The most significant and profound virtue of mankind is not their intellectual capacity, nor their technological skill or achievements, neither their advanced modern expression nor their eloquence, but the capacity of the individual to comprehend and reflect the impression and image and likeness of God! Your greatest feature is not your attractive face or your sexy body, nor your fame or fancy car, but his glory, his opinion reflecting in you! This persuasion becomes an awareness within you, which makes your life irresistibly attractive! We can afford ourselves the luxury to entertain the thoughts of God concerning us, exclusively. We are the god-kind by design! This is what Jesus revealed and redeemed!

"I say, You are gods, sons of the Most High, all of you." Psa 82:6 It is amazing that Jesus said that to a group of fanatical Pharisees who threatened to kill him for saying, "I and the Father are one!" John 10:30

God has no competition, you are his idea to begin with! Jesus is proof that God did not make a mistake when he made you!

The greatest insult to the religious ear is the fact that Jesus could say as a man, "I and the Father are one!" The conclusion of his triumphant act on the cross is now realized! John 14:20 "In that day you will know that I am in my Father, and you in me and I in you!"

Image and likeness would have no relevance if that was not what Jesus both revealed and redeemed in human form! The result? Eternal romance!

This was the critical moment when, in the movie, "The Lion King" Simba discovered his true identity when he saw his Father's face mirrored in him.

David echoes this in Psalm 23:2,3, "By the waters of reflection, my soul remembers who I am!" Also in Psalm 16:11. "In your presence is fullness of joy!" (TheHebrew word translated, "presence" means face to face, I am mirrored in you.) Fullness of joy is to see the Father's face mirrored in the reflection of your own eyes.

James, the younger brother of Jesus writes about lost and found identity: From the first and the last verse of James chapter one, it appears that James sets his teaching up against the sense of a lost identity: the twelve scattered tribes, and the widows and the orphans.

To lose your land of heritage or your immediate family would be the greatest and most challenging test or temptation anyone can face: "to forget what manner of man you are." *(Jas 1:24, Deut 32:18.)*

As the flesh-and-blood brother of Jesus, there was a time when neither he nor any of his family believed in Jesus. *(John 7:5)* It was only after the resurrection when Jesus appeared to him that the truth dawned on him, that his brother Jesus was indeed the one who all the rumors and prophetic pointers throughout time said he was! Jesus is God unveiled in flesh, the incarnate Word who redeemed the lost identity of mankind in his death and resurrection!

Man began in God! We are not merely the desire of a parent, we are the desire of God. Mankind shares a common origin, the *boulomai*, the affectionate desire and deliberate resolve of God, the Father of lights, with whom there is no distortion or hidden agenda. The unveiling of mankind's redemption also reveals our true genesis; we are God's personal invention. We are *anouthen*, from above. We are perfect and complete and lacking in nothing. God's Sabbath is the celebration of our perfection, both by design and redemption. "Every good and perfect gift comes from above, *(anouthen)* from the Father of lights with whom there is no variableness and no shadow due to change, he brought us forth by the Word of truth."

John sees the same genesis. He only begins to write when he is already more than 90 years old. Unlike Luke and Matthew, he skips the genealogies of Joseph, he declares, "In the beginning was the Word, what God was, the Word was, and the Word became flesh. He sees that the destiny of the Word was not the book, but human life! God finding accurate expression of himself, his image and likeness revealed in human form. Genesis 1:26 lives again; man is standing tall in the stature of the invisible God. "If you have seen me, you have seen the Father!" "Unless a man is born from above *(anouthen)*, he cannot see the Kingdom of God." The kingdom of God *(the reign of God's image and likeness in human life)* is made visible again on earth as it is in heaven; tangible in human form. *(Jn 3:3)*

In John 3 Nicodemus discovers that his irresistable attraction to Jesus was because of the fact that our natural birth is not our beginning! We come from above! God knew us before he formed us in our mother's womb! [Jer 1:5] If man did not come from above, the heavenly realm would offer no attraction to him. In our make-up we are the god-kind with an appetite for more than what bread and the senses could satisfy us with. We are designed to hunger for and feast from the Logos that comes from above. From a dimension where the original thought remains preserved and intact without contamination; the Logos that comes from his mouth is the unveiled mirror radiance of our authentic origin, quickening and sustaining the life of our design. "No one ascended into heaven, who did not also descend from heaven, even the son of man." *(Jn 3:13)*

Paul celebrates the same theme in Galatians 1:15 God's eternal [1]love dream separated me from my mother's womb; his grace became my [2]identity. *([1]eudokeo: his beautiful intention; the well done opinion. My mother's womb, my natural lineage and identity as son of Benjamin. [2]kaleo, to surname, to summon by name.)* 1:16 This is the heart of the gospel that I proclaim; it began with an unveiling of sonship [1]in me, freeing me to announce the same sonship [2]in the masses of non-Jewish people. I felt no immediate urgency to compare notes with those who were familiar with Christ from a mere historic point of view. *(The Greek text is quite clear, "It pleased the Father to reveal his son in me in order that I may proclaim him in the nations!" [1]en emoi, in me, and [2]en ethnos, in the Gentile nations, or the masses of non Jewish people! Not 'among' the Gentiles as most translations have it. Later when Barnabas is sent to investigate the conversion of the Greeks in Acts 11, instead of reporting his findings to the HQ in Jerusalem, he immediately finds Paul, knowing that Paul's gospel is the revelation of the mystery of Christ in the nations. Col.1:27. No wonder then that those believers were the first to be called Christians, or Christ-like!)*

Paul reminds the Greek philosophers in Acts 17 that we live and move and have our being in God; humankind is indeed the offspring of God. He is quoting from their own writings, Aratus, who lived 300 BC. The incorruptible seed of sonship is as much in every man as the seed is already in all soil, even in the desert, waiting for the rain to awaken and ignite its life!

Therefore, Paul did not immediately consult with flesh and blood. He deliberately avoided the opportunity to get to know Jesus from a human point of view by visiting the eleven disciples who were still alive and living in Jerusalem. They could have informed him first-hand about the life, ministry, parables, and miracles of Jesus. *(2 Cor 5:16)* But Paul does not make mention in any of his writings even of a single parable Jesus told or miracle he performed, because his mandate and revelation was not to merely relate Christ in history, but to reveal Christ in man.

Only three years later he returned briefly to Jerusalem specifically to visit Peter and James, the Lord's brother. *(Gal 1:18, 19.)* One is not surprized to discover that the first believers ever to be called Christians were the Greeks in Antioch who sat under Paul's ministry. *(Acts 11)*

Jesus has come to reveal that the son of man is the son of God. "If you have seen me you have seen the Father! Mat 23:9 "Call no man your father on earth, for you have one Father, who is in heaven." He says to Peter, "Flesh-and-blood cannot reveal to you who the son of man is, but my Father who is in heaven." He reveals in the man Jesus that mankind is the offspring of God. Blessed are you, Simon son of Jonah, I give you a new name that reveals your original identity: you are Rock! *(petros, hewn out of the rock, petra [Isa 51:1, Deut 32:3, 4, 18]. This revelation is the rock foundation that I will build my identity upon, (my image and likeness) and the strong gates of hades, (ha + ideis, not to see) that trapped man into the walled city of the senses will not prevail against the voice that surnames and summons man again. Mt 16:13, 17. Church, ekklesia, from ek, denoting source or origin and klesia from kaleo, to surname or identify by name.)*

What James, Peter and Paul had in common was an understanding that Jesus came to reveal and redeem man's authentic spirit identity, mankind is the godkind.

Of his own inspiration, God brought us forth by the word of truth… for anyone to hear this word, is to see the face of his birth reflected as in a mirror.

James 1:18 "It was his delightful resolve to give birth to us; we were conceived by the unveiled logic of God. (The Word of truth.) We lead the exhibition of his handiwork, like first fruits introducing the rest of the harvest he anticipates. James 1:23 The difference between a mere spectator and a performer is that both of them hear the same voice and perceive in its message the face of their own genesis reflected as in a mirror; 1:24 they realize that they are looking at themselves, but for the one it seems just too good to be true, he departs (back to his old way of seeing himself) never giving another thought to the man he saw there in the mirror. 1:25 The other one is mesmerized by what he sees, he is captivated by the effect of a law that frees man from the obligation to the old written code that restricted him to his own efforts and willpower. No distraction or contradiction can dim the impact of what he sees in that mirror concerning the law of perfect liberty (the law of faith) that now frees him to get on with the act of living the life (of his original design.) He finds a new spontaneous lifestyle; the poetry of practical living. (Understanding the mirror identity of man perfects the law of liberty; look deep enough into that law of faith that you may see there in its perfection a portrait that so resembles the original that he becomes distinctly visible in the spirit of your mind and in the face of every man you behold.

Mesmerized, parakupto, from para, a preposition indicating close proximity, a thing proceeding from a sphere of influence, with a suggestion of union of place of residence, to sprung from its author and giver, originating from, denoting the point from which an action originates, intimate connection, and kupto, to bend, stoop down to view at close scrutiny, parameno, to remain under the influence. Freedom, eleutheria, without obligation.)

The word of truth is the word that holds the blueprint of man's original design, and declares man's authentic value. To see yourself this way, and then to go away and forget who you really are when you face contradiction, is to deceive yourself. This illusion is man's biggest enemy! To forget what manner of man you are is such a waste of precious life! 2 Peter 1:8,9. It is like being blind and short sighted to everything God gifted us with. For a moment the contradiction seems more credible than the truth. Embrace the truth.

To struggle to do, means to fail to see. Doing spontaneously is directly related to perceiving and realising the integrity of your individual identity and value. Doing follows conclusion.

I am, therefore I can!

Gazing at the reflection of the face of your genesis redeemed in Christ reveals perfection as in a mirror and ignites the law of perfect liberty. It is almost like picking up an old coin that has become crusted over with dirt and time, and then upon cleaning the coin, to discover the original inscription to be still intact! The lost coin never lost its original image or value.

Any sincere student of music would sensitively seek to so capture and interpret the piece, not to distract from the original thought and inspiration of the composer.

To form an accurate conclusion in the study of our origin would involve a peering over the Creator's shoulder as it were, in order to gaze through his eyes and marvel at his anticipation.

The word of truth accurately preserves his original idea in the resonance of our hearts.

Jesus encouraged a level of hearing that would result in spontaneous action. He compared this to a man digging deep until the foundation of the house he builds, would rest upon rock. This house can withstand any size storm or onslaught. The rock communicates its strength of character through the foundation, which makes the strength of the structure equal to the rock it is founded upon. Matt. 7:24-27.

Discover your identity, "Look to the Rock from which you were hewn and the quarry from which you were dug!" Is. 51:1. The Rock preserves the mould and blueprint of our original design.

The greatness of the Master craftsman is displayed in his workmanship: "Ascribe greatness to our God, the Rock; his work is perfect!" (Deut.32:4) "We are his workmanship, created in Christ Jesus." We are engineered by his design; he manufactured us in Christ. (Greek, poeima, we are his poem, God finds inspired expression of Christ in us.) We are fully fit to do good; we are equipped to give attractive evidence to his likeness in us in everything we do. (God has done everything necessary to restore spontaneous and effortless expression of his Royal character in us in our everyday lifestyle.) Eph. 2:10. "Like living stones be yourselves built into a spiritual house…"1 Peter 2:5. "When the house was built, it was with stone perfectly prepared in the quarry; so that neither hammer nor axe nor any tool of iron was heard in the temple, while it was being built.' 1 Kings 6:7. The death and resurrection of Jesus is the quarry wherein God perfectly redeemed his original image and likeness again in human form!

God's Sabbath is a celebration of perfection!

Love, joy, peace, patience, kindness, goodness, integrity, humility and self-control are not fragile, fading emotions, produced by willpower. They are the fruit of what you know in your spirit to be true about you. Fruit is the effortless, spontaneous expression of the character of the tree. This knowledge ignites the law of perfect liberty. "Against such, there is no law." Galatians 5:13-15,22,23. These character qualities are not rewards for the most diligent and disciplined among us, neither are they "pie in the sky, wishful thinking" illusions. They reflect in fact the very nature of our authentic design.

2 Cor 4:4 The god of this world has blinded the minds of the unbelievers, to keep them from seeing the light of the gospel of the glory of Christ, who is the likeness of God. (An unbeliever is anyone who disagrees with God about their true perfection revealed and redeemed in Christ)

God desires to reveal within you a treasure of immeasurable value. A wealth that surpasses all consciousness of lack! Only the light of the gospel can reveal this. John 1:4 His life is the light that defines our lives.

John 1:9 A new day for humanity has come. The authentic light of life that illuminates everyone was about to dawn in the world! *(This day would begin our calendar and record the fact that human history would forever be divided into before and after Christ. The incarnation would make the image of God visible in human form. In him who is the blueprint of our lives there is more than enough light to displace the darkness in every human life. He is the true light that enlightens every man! [Col 1:15; 2:9, 10; 2 Cor 4:6])*

There is such a large difference between wishful thinking and truthful being. So many people are trapped in the ignorance of striving to become something they already are by design and by redemption. Nothing will please you more than to know and believe the true testimony of you. 1 John 5:9. The most attractive life you can live is a life conscious and persuaded of this.

Like a small rudder steers and directs a massive ship, so our thoughts and conversation about ourselves dictate our day and destiny on the ocean of life.

Window-shopping only teases you with dreams and desires beyond your reach. Gazing into the mirror, however, reveals the essence and integrity of your true nature, the image and likeness of God. 2 Corinthians 3:18. See within that sacred focus the face of your birth, conceived in his thought before time began; now redeemed again in Christ.

To strive to obtain love, peace and joy etc. or to pray to God to give you these qualities is wasted religious energy. "My people perish through lack of knowledge..." Hosea 4:6.

Prayer doesn't have power in itself! The perception exists that God needs to be talked into doing things for us. It is not how long or loud you pray, it is about realizing his presence and provision within you; this is what sets you free to be who you are redeemed to be. The more aware we become of God in us, the more overwhelmed we are with a sense of total fulfilment and completeness; needs disappear into insignificance. He is not a God who is a far off, he is Emmanuel!

Nothing you can seek to do or wish and pray for could qualify you more for life. Nothing can make you more attractive or your life more significant than to simply become aware of his nature and presence in you and his favour towards you mirrored in the finished work of Christ.

Our prayers and worship now blend in harmony with the eternal reflection and ascension of earth's praise, the adoration not of men only but of all created things. E. Goudge.

Like bird-song or the fragrance of flowers and incense, every minute molecule and vibrating atom has a voice, saluting the Maker. Listen up! Beyond the silence their voice echoes like the sound of many waters.

THE INCARNATION

Jesus is the image of the invisible God! Any idea we might have of God that is unlike Jesus is not God! Col 1:15 In him the image and likeness of God is made visible in human life in order that every one may recognize their true origin in him. He is the firstborn of every creature. *(What darkness veiled from us he unveiled. In him we clearly see the mirror reflection of our original life. The son of his love gives accurate evidence of his image in human form. God can never again be invisible!)*

John 1:1 To go back to the very ¹beginning is to find the ²Word already ³present there. The ²Logic of God defines the only possible place where humankind can trace their ⁴genesis. The Word is ³I am; God's eternal ²eloquence echoes and ⁵concludes in him. The Word equals God. *(¹arche, to be first in order, time, place or rank. The Word, ²logos, was ⁵"with" God; here John uses the Greek preposition ⁵pros, which indicates direction, forward to; that is toward the destination of the relation. Face-to-face. "For as the rain and the snow come down from heaven and return, having accomplished their purpose (canceling distance and saturating the earth and awakening the seed in the soil), so shall my word be that proceeds from my mouth." [Isa 55:10, 11]). The destiny of the word is always to return face to face.*

Three times in this sentence John uses the imperfect of ³eimi, namely ³en, to be, which conveys no idea of origin for God or for the Logos, but simply continuous existence. Quite a different verb egeneto, "became," appears in John 1:14 for the beginning of the Incarnation of the Logos. See the distinction sharply drawn in John 8:58, "before Abraham was born (¹genesthai from egeneto) I am" (eimi, timeless existence.)

John 1:2 The beginning mirrors the Word face to face with God. *(Nothing that is witnessed in the Word distracts from who God is. "If you have seen me, you have seen the Father." [John 14:9])*

John 1:3 The Logos is the source; everything commences in him. He remains the exclusive Parent reference to their genesis. There is nothing original, except the Word!

John 1:4 His life is the light that defines our lives. *(In his life man discovers the light of life.)*

John 1:5 The darkness was pierced and could not comprehend or diminish this light. *(Darkness represents man's ignorance of his redeemed identity and innocence [Isa 9:2-4, Isa 60:1-3, Eph 3:18, Col 1:13-15].)*

John 1:9 A new day for humanity has come. The authentic light of life that illuminates everyone was about to dawn in the world! *(This day would begin our calendar and record the fact that human history would forever be divided into before and after Christ. The incarnation would make the image of God visible in human form. In him who is the blueprint of our lives there is more than enough light to displace the darkness in every human life. He is the true light that enlightens every man! [Col 1:15; 2:9, 10; 2 Cor 4:6])*

John 1:10 Although no one took any notice of him, he was no stranger to the world; he always was there and is himself the author of all things.

John 1:11 It was not as though he arrived on a foreign planet; he came to his own, yet his own did not [1]recognize him. *(Ps 24:1, "The earth is the Lord's and the fullness thereof, the world and those who dwell in it [RSV]." The word, [1]paralambano, comes from **para**, a preposition indicating close proximity, a thing proceeding from a sphere of influence, with a suggestion of union of place of residence, to have sprung from its author and giver, originating from, denoting the point from which an action originates, intimate connection; and **lambano**, to comprehend, grasp, to identify with.)*

John 1:12 Everyone who [1]realizes their association in him, [6]convinced that he is their [2]original life and that [7]his name defines them, [5]in them he [3]endorses the fact that they are indeed his [4]offspring, [2]begotten of him; he [3]sanctions the legitimacy of their sonship. *(The word often translated, to receive, [1]lambano, means to comprehend, grasp, to identify with. This word suggests that even though he came to his own, there are those who do not [1]grasp their true [2]origin revealed in him, and like the many Pharisees they behave like children of a foreign father, the father of lies [Jn 8: 44]. Neither God's legitimate fatherhood of man nor his ownership is in question; man's indifference to his true [2]origin is the problem. This is what the Gospel addresses with utmost clarity in the person of Jesus Christ. Jesus has come to introduce man to himself again; humanity has forgotten what manner of man he is by design! [Jas 1:24, Deut 32:18, Ps 22:27].*

The word, [2]genesthai [aorist tense, which is like a snapshot taken of an event that has already taken place], from ginomai, to become [See 1:3]. The Logos is the source; everything commences in him. He remains the exclusive Parent reference to their genesis. There is nothing original, except the Word! Man began in God [see also Acts 17:28]. "He has come to give us understanding to know him who is true and to realize that we are in him who is true." [1 Jn 5:20].)

The word, [3]exousia, often translated "power;" as in, he gave "power" to [2]become children of God, is a compound word; from ek, always denoting origin or source and eimi, I am; thus, out of I am! This gives [3]legitimacy and authority to our sonship; [4]teknon, translated as offspring, child.

*"He has given," [5]didomi, in this case to give something to someone that already belongs to them; thus, to return. The fact that they already are his own, born from above, they have their [2]beginning and their being in him is now confirmed in their realizing it! Convinced, [6]pisteo; [7]his name **onoma**, defines man [see Eph 3:15].*

"He made to be their true selves, their child-of-God selves." — The Message)

John 1:13 These are they who discover their genesis in God beyond their natural conception! Man began in God. We are not the invention of our parents!

John 1:14 Suddenly the invisible eternal Word takes on [1]visible form! The Incarnation! In him, and now confirmed in us! The most accurate tangible display of God's eternal thought finds expression in human life! The Word became a human being; we are his address; he resides in us! He [2]captivates our gaze! The glory we see there is not a religious replica; he is the [3]authentic begotten son. *([3]monogenes begotten only by the Father and not by the flesh; in him we recognize our true beginning).* The [4]glory *(that Adam lost)* returns in fullness! Only [5]grace can communicate truth in such complete context! *(In him we discover that we are not here by chance or accident or by the desire of an earthly parent, neither are we the product of a mere physical conception; we exist by the expression of God's desire to reveal himself in the flesh. His eternal invisible Word, his Spirit-thought, [1]became flesh, [1]ginomai, as in be born and [2]theaomai, meaning to gaze upon, to perceive. We saw his glory, [4]doxa, the display of his opinion, the glory as of the original, authentic begotten of the Father, full of grace and truth. He is both the "only begotten," [3]monogenes; as in the authentic original mold, as well as the first born from the dead [Col 1:18, 1 Pet 1:3]. He is the revelation of our completeness.*

And of his fullness have we all received, grace against grace, [5]garin anti garitos, grace undeserved. For the law was given through Moses, grace and truth came through Jesus Christ. He who is in the bosom of the Father, the only original, authentic begotten of the Father; he is our guide who accurately declares and interprets the invisible God within us. Interesting that the revelation of the Incarnation in verse 14 doesn't follow verse 2 or 3, but verse 12 and 13! Genesis 1:26 is redeemed!)

John 1:15 John the Baptist raised his voice to announce emphatically that Jesus was what his ministry and prophetic message were all about. He declared that Jesus, though younger than him, ranks above him and was "born" before him, since he always was!

John 1:16 He is the source of our completeness. [1]Grace against grace! *([1]garin anti garitos, grace undeserved. Grace prevailed against the tide of darkness due to Adam's fall. His fullness is the source of all that grace communicates as our portion, against all odds!)*

John 1:17 Against the stark backdrop of the law, with Moses representing the condemned state of mankind, Jesus Christ unveils grace and truth! *(He is the life of our design redeemed in human form).*

John 1:18   Until this moment God remained invisible to man; now the [1]authentic begotten son, (*[1]monogenes, begotten only of God*) the blueprint of man's design who represents the innermost being of God, the son who is in the bosom of the father, brings him into full view! He is the [2]official authority qualified to announce God! He is our guide who accurately declares and interprets the invisible God within us. (*Official guide, [2]eksegesato, from ek, preposition denoting source, and hegeomai, the strengthened form of ago, to lead as a shepherd leads his sheep; thus hegeomai means to be officially appointed in a position of authority.*

2 Cor 4:18 It is the unseen eternal realm within us that has our full attention and captivates our gaze!

2 Cor 3:18 The days of window-shopping are over! In him every face is unveiled. In gazing with wonder at the blueprint likeness of God displayed in human form we suddenly realize that we are looking at ourselves! Every feature of his image is mirrored in us! This is the most radical transformation engineered by the Spirit of the Lord; we are led from an inferior mind-set to the revealed endorsement of our authentic identity.)

The destiny of the Word was not a book; it has always been the incarnation. The invisible image and likeness of God is made visible again in human life. God cannot get any closer to mankind than what he did in Christ. The Word became flesh.

Seven hundred years before Christ the prophet Isaiah proclaimed: "In the wilderness prepare the highway of the Lord; every valley shall be lifted up, every mountain and hill be made low, the uneven ground shall become level, every crooked place shall be made straight, even the rough places shall be made smooth. And the glory of the Lord shall be revealed. And all flesh shall see it together." Is.40:4,5, Luk3:4-6. The wilderness is the fruit of the curse, it was never meant to be man's journey or destiny. Israel was trapped there because they believed a lie about themselves. Num.13:33.

God takes pleasure in mankind. His reference exceeds anything that could possibly disqualify man. In Christ he has broken down every wall of hostility and every excuse we have to feel distant from him.

In the incarnation God speaks a language that all flesh understands. In Christ God reveals the new and living way: The word made flesh makes the invisible God visible and in the same breath reflects the authentic mirror image of man. Col.1:15-23.

The Incarnation is God's highway! Every definition of distance was cancelled in Christ. Now any excuse we could possibly have to feel neglected or distanced from God or to continue in a life of spiritual drought, isolation, sin, unworthiness, guilt and inferiority is cancelled. Mankind is no longer trapped in a wilderness. Jesus is the way of escape. From believing the lie to knowing the truth about ourselves! "As he is so are we in this world!" 1 Jhn 4:17

In John 14:2 and 20 Jesus prophesies how through his death and resurrection he would prepare a place for us so that we may be where he is, one with his Father, wrapped up in union with him. Jesus was not about to become a building contractor in heaven. He is not in the mansion building-business, as some translations will imply! In his death and resurrection he prepared a place for us of restored intimate oneness with himself and the Father in spirit and in truth.

"If you have seen me you have seen the Father." John 14:2,8-12. "I and the Father are one." John 10:30

Jesus reveals that God is not separate from man; he is Emmanuel. God can never be God without man; we bear his image and likeness. James 3:9, Luk 20:24.

Sometimes the thought of a Triune God confuses us. The Incarnation did not interrupt or divide God's oneness. In some of the Pentecostal and Charismatic traditions we have taught on the Holy Spirit in a way that has almost distracted from God the Father and God the Son. When Jesus introduces us to the Holy Spirit, he reveals him as the mirror of himself in the same order that the Son mirrors the Father! He says in John 14:18 "I will not leave you orphans; I will come to you! The mirror image gives such an accurate account; the one reveals the other, without distraction! He is eternal Oneness; the Incarnation reveals man's co-inclusion in the same oneness! "In that day (the day of redemption) you will know that I m in my Father and you in me and I in you!" John 14:20.

In a symphony orchestra, every individual instrument reflects the other; the music is one. "For unto us a child is born, and his name shall be called: ...the everlasting Father!" Is.9:6. The revelation of God as Father, the true Origin of man, is the central theme of the Gospel. All that Jesus is and accomplished confirms this. He has shown us the Father in such a way that we cannot but know that he is in the Father and we are in him and he is in us! "We are in him who is true!" 1 Jhn 5:20

2 Cor 3:17 The Lord and the Spirit are one; his Lordship sanctions our freedom. A freedom from rules chiseled in stone to the voice of our redeemed design echoing in our hearts! 2 Cor 3:18 The days of window-shopping are over! In him every face is [1]unveiled. In [2]gazing with wonder at the [5]blueprint likeness of God displayed in human form we sudden-

ly realize that we are looking at ourselves! Every feature of his [3]image is [2]mirrored in us! This is the most radical [4]transformation engineered by the Spirit of the Lord; we are led [6]from an inferior [5]mind-set to the revealed [5]endorsement of our authentic identity. Mankind is his [5]glory! *(The word, [1]anakekalumeno, is a perfect passive participle from anakalupto; ana, a preposition denoting upward, to return again, and kalupto, to uncover, unveil. The word, [2]katoptrizomenoi, is the present middle participle from katoptrizomai, meaning to gaze into a reflection, to mirror oneself. The word [4]metamorphumetha is a present passive indicative from metamorpho; meta, together with, and meros, form. [The word commonly translated for sin, hamartia, is the opposite of this as ha, means without, and meros, form.] The word, [3]eikon, translates as exact resemblance, image and likeness; eikon always assumes a prototype, that which it not merely resembles, but from that which it is drawn; [5]doxa, glory, translates as mind-set, opinion from dokeo, authentic thought. Changed 'from glory to glory', apo doxes eis doxan; eis, a point reached in conclusion; [6]apo, away from, meaning away from the glory that previously defined us, i.e. our own achievements or disappointments, to the glory of our original design that now defines us. [Paul writes in Romans 1:17 about the unveiling of God's righteousness and then says it is from faith to faith. Here he does not use the word apo, but the preposition, ek, which always denotes source or origin.] Two glories are mentioned in this chapter; the glory of the flesh, and the unfading glory of God's image and likeness redeemed in us. The fading glory represented in the dispensation of the law of Moses is immediately superseded by the unveiling of Christ in us! Some translations of this scripture reads, "we are being changed from glory to glory." This would suggest that change is gradual and will more than likely take a lifetime, which was the typical thinking that trapped Israel for forty years in the wilderness of unbelief! We cannot become more than what we already are in Christ. We do not grow more complete; we simply grow in the knowledge of our completeness! [See Col 3:10] We are not changed "from one degree of glory to another," or step by step. How long does it take the beautiful swan to awaken to the truth of its design? The ugly duckling was an illusion! Whatever it was that endorsed the 'ugly duckling' mindset, co-died together with Christ!)*

2 Cor 4:1 Since we are employed by the mercy of God, and not by our own qualifications, quitting is not an option.

2 Cor 4:2 We have renounced hidden agendas *(employing a little bit of the law in an attempt to "balance" out grace)*; we have distanced ourselves from any obscure craftiness to manipulate God's word to make it mean what it does not say! With truth on open display in us, we highly recommend our lives to every one's [1]conscience! Truth finds its most authentic and articulate expression in human life. This beats any doctrinal debate! *(It is our passion for all to see what is so completely obvious in the mirror of our redeemed likeness and innocence! [1]Conscience in Latin means to know together; in the Greek, [1]suneido, translates as joint seeing; which is the opposite of hades, not to see.)*

2 Cor 4:3 If our message seems vague to anyone, it is not because we are withholding something from certain people! It is just because some are so stubborn in their efforts to uphold an outdated system that they don't see it! They are all equally found in Christ but they prefer to remain lost in the cul-de-sac language of the law!

2 Cor 4:4 The survival and self-improvement programs of the [1]religious systems of this world veil the minds of the unbelievers; exploiting their ignorance about their true origin and their redeemed innocence. The veil of unbelief obstructs a person's view and keeps one from seeing what the light of the gospel so clearly reveals: the [2]glory of God is the image and likeness of our Maker redeemed in human form; this is what the gospel of Christ is all about. *(The god of this [1]aion, age, refers to the religious systems and governing structures of this world. The unbelief that neutralized Israel in the wilderness was the lie that they believed about themselves; "We are grasshoppers, and the 'enemy' is a giant beyond any proportion!" [Num 13:33, Josh 2:11, Heb 4:6] "They failed to possess the promise due to unbelief." The blueprint [2]doxa, glory of God, is what Adam lost on humanity's behalf. [See Eph 4:18])*

2 Cor 4:5 Even though we recommend ourselves with great confidence, it is not with arrogance; we do not preach ourselves! We preach Christ Jesus the Lord; we are salvation junkies; employed by Jesus for your sakes.

2 Cor 4:6 The light source is founded in the same God who said, "Light, be!" And light shone out of darkness! He lit the lamp in our understanding so that we may clearly recognize the features of his likeness in the face of Jesus Christ reflected within us. *(The same God who bade light shine out of darkness has kindled a light in our hearts, whose shining is to make known his glory as he has revealed it in the features of Jesus Christ. — Knox Translation)*

2 Cor 4:7 We have discovered this treasure where it was hidden all along, in these frail skin-suits made of clay. We take no credit for finding it there! It took the enormous power of God in the achievement of Christ to rescue our minds from the lies it believed. *("The kingdom of heaven is like treasure hidden in an agricultural field, which a man found and covered up; then in his joy he goes and sells all that he has and buys that field." [Mt 13:44] God invested all that he has in the redeeming of our original value! He rescued the life of our design. Our inner life hosts the treasure of the life of our design. Jesus said in John 7:37,38, "If you believe that I am what the scriptures are all about, you will know that you are what I am all about and rivers of living water will gush out of your innermost being!")*

"In Christ there is all of God in a human body!" Kenneth Taylor. *"It is in him that we find our completion; he is the fountainhead from which all dominion and power proceed."* Knox. Col 2:9-10. *"It is in him that God gives a full and complete expression of himself in a human body. Moreover, your own completeness*

is only realised in him!" Phillips. "Of his fullness have we all received." John 1:14

The vessel takes its value from the treasure it holds! "We have this treasure in clay pots." God sees your flesh as a worthy vessel! I once sold my son's Isuzu for R18 000. When I delivered the vehicle the man paid me with the cash in an old brown envelope. I folded the envelope and stuck it in my pocket. The Khaki pants I wore, I bought at Mr Price for R79.99; they were now suddenly worth R18 079.99.

This truth and its fully realised consequence will conquer the world!

"And the glory of the Lord shall be revealed and all flesh shall see it together!" Isaiah 40:5. All flesh shall discover their true glory revealed within them! 2 Cor 4:7 We have discovered this treasure where it was hidden all along, in these frail skin-suits made of clay. We take no credit for finding it there! It took the enormous power of God in the achievement of Christ to rescue our minds from the lies it believed. (*"The kingdom of heaven is like treasure hidden in an agricultural field, which a man found and covered up; then in his joy he goes and sells all that he has and buys that field." [Mt 13:44] God invested all that he has in the redeeming of our original value! He rescued the life of our design. Our inner life hosts the treasure of the life of our design. Jesus said in John 7:37,38, "If you believe that I am what the scriptures are all about, you will know that you are what I am all about and rivers of living water will gush out of your innermost being!")* "The knowledge of the glory of the Lord shall cover the earth even as the waters cover the sea." Habakkuk 2:14.

"The eye is the lamp of the body! If the eye is focussed (Greek, *haplous*, from *hama* + *pleko*, intertwined) the whole body will be full of light." The revelation of the Incarnation will enlighten your whole person. Matthew 6:22. The true light that enlightens every man has come! John 1:9

In Matthew 16 we read how Simon's name was changed to Rock (Peter) when he it was revealed to him that Jesus, the son of man was the Messiah, the Son of the living God. The mission of the Messiah was to redeem mankind's sonship! He revealed that the son of man was the son of God!

Everyone knew Simon by his surname, son of Jonah; by revelation he discovered that flesh and blood does not define man's true sonship; Jesus was the mirror of mankind's authentic origin. The son of man was indeed son of God. Man began in God and not in his mother's womb! The son of man was hewn from the Rock of Ages! Deut 32:18, Isaiah 51:1, 1Kings 6:7.

We have forgotten the Rock that begot us; we have forgotten what manner of people we are! Jesus has come to introduce humanity to their true origin. He came to introduce us to ourselves again.

54

Having contemplated and discussed the implication of such a revelation at length, the Rock (Peter) and his two fisherman-partners, James and John are invited to join Jesus six days later on a high mountain. Matthew 17:1-9. Three illiterate fisherman are about to witness the greatest spectacle! Suddenly on reaching the summit, Jesus is transfigured before them. His face began to shine like the sun and his clothes became dazzling white like light; just then there appeared before them Moses and Elijah in conversation with Jesus. Six days after Simon discovers his own new identity in the revelation of the Christ, God reveals man in his image, just like he did on the sixth day in Genesis chapter one, when, for the first time in the history of the universe, the invisible God showed his likeness in a body of flesh and blood.

In Jesus the fullness of God is realised in a human body! Col 1:15, Col 2:9,10. Just to prove and confirm to Peter that he was right in seeing that the son of man was indeed the son of God, for a moment he briefly burst through the confines of flesh, proving that the human body was not an inferior tabernacle to contain God.

Adam and Eve lost the glory and fell away from that order of life; they became dwarfed and dormant in their minds. Isa 55:8-10. But here in Christ, that same glory is revealed again. Jesus is the full expression in one Person of all the fragments of God's thought concerning man's original design and identity.

Hebrews 1:1 Throughout ancient times God spoke in many fragments and glimpses of prophetic thought to our fathers. Heb 1:2 Now, the sum total of his conversation with man has finally culminated in a son. He is the official heir of all things. He is, after all, the author of the ages. Jesus is what has been on the tip of the Father's tongue all along!

This time it is not a reflection of the image and likeness of God in a separate person, but God himself in the flesh. A new eternal seventh day is about to dawn: the Sabbath of the same substance that God celebrated when his faith saw the triumph of the cross! The Lamb was slain before the fall. Man is now invited to join God in his rest; to see what God sees and to co-know with him.

God does not grow weary or tired; his rest is so much more than a special holy day; it is the celebration of the completeness of his ageless dream; the Master Craftsman added his final touch, the masterpiece says it all. "We are his workmanship, created in Christ Jesus." Eph 2:10. (Greek, *poema, his poem!*)

"He rests in his love, and spins around in delight and jubilant joy at the thought of you!" Zeph 3:17.

The Greek word for love, agape is a compound word from ago, which means to lead as a shepherd leads his sheep, and pao, which means rest! His love leads me into his rest. Agape is Psalm 23 in one word. "By the waters of reflection my soul remembers who I am."

"Today if you hear my voice, do not harden your hearts." Heb 3:13 Instead, ¹remind one another daily of your true identity; make today count! Do not allow callousness of heart to cheat any of you for even a single day out of your allotted portion. *("To encourage one another daily," from the word, ¹parakaleo, from para, a preposition indicating close proximity, a thing proceeding from a sphere of influence, with a suggestion of union of place of residence, to have sprung from its author and giver, originating from, denoting the point from which an action originates, intimate connection, and kaleo, to identify by name, to surname. Jesus introduces the Holy Spirit in the same capacity, parakletos [Jn 14:16] Greek, hamartia, sin,without form, or allotted portion. Sin would be anything that distracts from the awareness of our likeness.)*

Heb 3:14 What we have become in our union with Christ must be taken to its ultimate conclusion. Do not cancel out your confident start by making a poor finish. *(Starting in faith then going back to the law of works.)* Heb 3:15 Every day is an extension of God's today; hear his voice, do not harden your heart. The stubborn rebellion of Israel brought them nowhere. Heb 3:16 The same people who experienced God's mighty act of deliverance out of Egypt under the leadership of Moses were the very ones who rebelled. Heb 3:17 They grieved him for forty years in the wilderness until they were reduced to nothing. Heb 3:18 God's invitation does not exclude anyone from possessing the promise of his ¹rest; their unbelief does. Persuasion cannot be compromized by unbelief. *(What God knows to be true about us cannot be compromized by our believing a lie about ourselves. Futile striving to become cannot match the bliss of discovering and celebrating who you alreday are by his design and redemption.)* Heb 3:19 The point is this: even though they survived by supernatural means in the wilderness for forty years, they failed to grasp what God had in mind for them. Their own unbelief disqualified them. *(They did not die because of an inferior salvation from Egypt; Pharaoh was taken out of the equation. They died because of unbelief, they believed a lie about themselves! [Num 13:33, Josh 2:11] Don't blame Pharaoh or the devil for your own unbelief!*

You can experience God's supernatural provision and protection and yet remain outside his rest. The ultimate proof of faith is not experience of the supernatural, but entering into his rest. His rest celebrates his perfect work; it finds its definition and reference in Genesis 1:31, 1 Kings 6:7 and Colossians 2:9, 10. He longs for you to discover your own completeness and perfection as seen from his point of view. His rest is sustained in you by what he sees, knows, and says about you in reference to the finished work of Christ. Jesus is what God believes about you.)

Heb 4:1 What a foolish thing it would be for us if we should now fail in a similar fashion to enter into the full consequences of our redemption.

Heb 4:2 The gospel we have heard today is the same gospel that was preached in the promise. *(Both share the same source, intent, and content; although the first was a mere shadow of the second).* God had mankind in mind all along; yet, because people lacked the persuasion by which the word could be ignited and brought to life in them, the promise did not profit them at all.

Heb 4:3 Faith *(not our own works)* realizes our entrance into God's rest *(into the result of his completed work).* Hear the echo of God's [1]cry though the ages, "Oh! If only they would enter into my rest." His rest celebrates perfection. His work is complete; the [2]fall of humanity did not flaw its perfection. *(Some translations read, "As I have sworn in my wrath" derived from [1]orge, meaning passionate desire, any strong outburst of emotion. "Oh! If only they would enter into my rest." First Adam failed to enter into God's finished work, and then Israel failed to enter into the consequence of their complete redemption out of Egypt, and as a result of their unbelief perished in the wilderness. Now let us not fail in the same manner to see the completed work of the Cross. How God desires for us to see the same perfection; what he saw when he first created man in his image and then again what he saw in the perfect obedience of his Son. God is not "in his rest" because he is exhausted, but because he is satisfied with what he sees and knows concerning us! He now invites us with [1]urgent persuasion to enter into what he sees. His rest was not at risk. "His works were finished from the foundation of the world." The word, apo, translates as away from, before and [2]katabalo, cast down, the fall of humanity, sometimes translated, foundation [see notes on Eph 1:4] "This association goes back to before the fall of the world, his love knew that he would present us again face to face before him in blameless innocence." The implications of the fall are completely cancelled out.)*

Heb 4:4 Scripture records the seventh day to be the prophetic celebration of God's perfect work. What God saw satisfied his scrutiny. *(Behold, it is very good, and God rested from all his work. [Gen 1:31, 2:2] God saw more than his perfect image in Adam, he also saw the Lamb and his perfect work of redemption! "The Lamb having been slain from the foundation of the world." [Rev 13:8] "That which has been is now; that which is to be, already has been" [Ecc 3:15])*

Heb 4:5 In Psalm 95 the same seventh day metaphor is reiterated: "O, that they would enter my rest!"

Heb 4:6 It is clear then that there is still an opportunity to enter into that rest which Israel failed to access because of their unbelief, even though they were the first to hear the good news of God's intention to restore mankind to the same Sabbath that Adam and Israel had lost. *(Both Adam and Israel believed a lie about themselves. [Num 13:33, Josh 2:11])*

Heb 4:7 So, now again many years later, he points specifically to an extended opportunity when he announces in David's prophecy, "Today when hearing my voice, do not do so with a calloused heart. Be faith sensitive."

Heb 4:8 If Joshua, who led the new generation of Israel out of the wilderness *(where their parents perished through unbelief)*, had succeeded in leading them into the rest that God intended, David would not so many years later have referred to yet another day. *(This moment still remains as an open invitation to mankind to enter into their rest: the living blueprint of their design. This confirms that the history of Israel was a mere shadow and prophetic type of that Promise that was yet to be fulfilled.)*

Heb 4:9 The conclusion is clear: the original rest is still in place for God's people. *(The people of this planet are the property of God [Ps 24:1])*

Heb 4:10 God's rest celebrates his finished work; whoever enters into God's rest immediately abandons his own efforts to compliment what God has already perfected. *(The language of the law is "do;" the language of grace is "done.")*

Heb 4:11 Let us therefore be prompt to understand and fully appropriate that rest and not fall again into the same trap that snared Israel in unbelief.

Heb 4:12 The message that God spoke to us in Christ is the most life giving and dynamic influence in us, cutting like a surgeon's scalpel, sharper than a soldier's sword, piercing to the deepest core of human conscience to the dividing of soul and spirit; ending the dominance of the sense realm and its neutralizing effect upon the human spirit. In this way man's spirit is freed to become the ruling influence again in the thoughts and intentions of the heart. The scrutiny of this word detects every possible disease, discerning the body's deepest secrets where joint and bone-marrow meet. *(The moment we cease from our own efforts to justify ourselves, by yielding to the integrity of the message that announces the success of the cross, God's word is triggered into action. What God spoke to us in sonship (the incarnation), radiates his image and likeness in our redeemed innocence. [Heb 1:1-3] This word powerfully penetrates and impacts our whole being; body, soul and spirit.)*

Heb 4:13 The whole person is thoroughly exposed to his scrutinizing gaze. Every creature's original form is on record in the Word. *(Representing God's desire to display his image and likeness in man.)*

Heb 4:14 In the message of the incarnation we have Jesus the Son of God representing humanity in the highest place of spiritual authority. That which God has spoken to us in him is his final word. It is echoed now in the declaration of our confession.

Heb 4:15 As High Priest he fully identifies with us in the context of our frail human lives. Having subjected it to close scrutiny, he proved that the human frame was master over sin. His sympathy with us is not to be seen as excusing weaknesses that are the result of a faulty design, but rather as a trophy to humanity. *(He is not an example for us but of us.)*

Heb 4:16 For this reason we can approach the authoritative throne of grace with bold utterance. We are welcome there in his embrace, and are [1]reinforced with immediate effect in times of trouble. *(The word, [1]boetheia, means to be reinforced, specifically a rope or chain for frapping a vessel in a storm.)*

Now is the fullness of time. Now is an eternal concept, not a time concept. Every moment in the history of man is God's now; also every moment in man's future is God's now! The moment the individual embraces his voice, the now of his eternal strategy begins to unfold. "From the day you heard and understood the grace of God in truth, you bore fruit!" Col.1:6.

Redemption is a reality. The cross was a success! Col 2:14 His body nailed to the cross hung there as the document of mankind's guilt; in dying our death he [1]deleted the detailed [2]hand-written [3]record of Adam's fall. Every [1]stain that sin left on our conscience was fully blotted out. *(The word, [1]exaleipho, comes from ek, out of, and aleipho, with a, as a particle of union, and liparos, to grease, to leave a stain; guilt was like a grease stain upon the conscience of fallen man. The word, [2]cheirographon, translates as hand-written. The word, [3]dogma, comes from dokeo, a thought pattern; thus thought patterns engraved by human experience of constant failure to do what the law required. In his personal handwriting man endorsed his own death sentence. The hands of fallen man struck the body of Jesus with the blows of their religious hatred and fury when they nailed his bloodied body to the tree; they did not realize that in the mystery of God's economy Jesus was the scapegoat of the entire human race! [Isa 53:4, 5] "The slate wiped clean, that old arrest warrant canceled and nailed to Christ's Cross." — The Message)*

Col 2:15 His brilliant victory made a public [1]spectacle of every [2]rule and [3]authority empowered by the fall of Adam. The [4]voice of the cross will never be silenced! *(The horror of the Cross is now the eternal trophy of God's triumph over sin! The cross stripped religion of its authority to manipulate man with guilt. Every accusation lost its power to continue to blackmail the human race. The word, [1]apekduomai, is translated from apo, away from, and ekduo, to be stripped of clothing; the religious facade that disguised the law of works as a means of defining man was openly defeated. The dominance of the tree of the knowledge of good and evil (poneros, hard work and labor) was ended. The word, [1]deikmatizo, means to exhibit in public. The word, [4]parresia, comes from pas, all and rheo, outspokenness, pouring forth speech.*

"He stripped all the spiritual tyrants in the universe of their sham authority at the Cross and marched them naked through the streets." — The Message

See commentary for 1 Corinthians 15:24, The complete conclusion in his work of redemption is celebrated in his yielding the full harvest of his reign to God the Father, having [1]brought to naught the law of works which supported every definition of dominion under the fall, including all [2]principalities, all [3]authority and every

4dynamic influence in society. [He brought to naught the law of works, 1katargeo, from kata, meaning intensity, and argos, meaning labor; thus free from all self effort to attempt to improve what God has already perfected in Christ. All principalities, 2arche, or chief ranks, i.e., kings, governors; this includes any governing system whereby one is ranked above the other on the basis of their performance or prefer- ence. All authority, 3exousia, comes from ek, denoting origin and eimi, I am; in this case, because of what I can do I am defined by what I can do better than you; therefore, I have authority over you. Every dynamic influence in society, 4dunamis, means power, in this case, willpower. Every government structure in society will be brought under the dominion of grace where the Christ life rules.]

In 1 Corinthians 2:7-8, We voice words of wisdom that was hidden in silence for timeless ages; a mystery unfolding God's Masterful plan whereby he would redeem his glory in man. Neither the politicians nor the theologians of the day had a clue about this mystery [of mankind's association in Christ]; if they did, they would never have crucified the Lord whose death redeemed our glory!)

Many sincere preachers continue to preach a defeated devil back into business! Jesus disarmed the claim and dominion of the Accuser. God's eternal verdict in man's favour is beyond dispute and a non-negotiable. "We are convinced that one has died for all, therefore all have died. From now on therefore, we no longer consider any man from a human point of view." 2 Corinthians 5:14,16. Out of all proportion to the effect of Adam's transgression, is the effect of the free gift of his grace in Christ Jesus. Rom. 5:15-19. (See Romans Revealed and 2 Cor 5:14-21 in the Mirror Bible)

As a Psalmist and worshipper of God, David knew the presence and the plan of God. The Spirit of Christ revealed to him the agony of Jesus's suffering on the cross a thousand years before the great historic event. He hears the cries of Jesus echoing mankind's sense of Godforsakeness, when in fact God never forsook mankind for a moment! The Shepherd never forsook the sheep! "We all like sheep have gone astray!" We have despised and rejected him, but he has not despised or abhorred the afflic- tion of the afflicted; and he has not hid his face from him; he has heard when he cried to him. "My God, my God why did you forsake me? Why are you so far away and do you not care to rescue me? Why do you seem to be deaf to the words of my groaning? I am poured out like water, and all my bones are out of joint; my heart is like wax, it is melted within my breast. My strength is dried up like a potsherd; and my tongue cleaves to my jaws. You laid me in the dust of death. Yea, dogs are round about me; a company of evildoers encircle me, they have pierced my hands and feet, I can count all my bones, they stare and gloat over me, they divide my garments among them, and for my raiment they cast lots! We have despised and rejected him, but he has not despised or abhorred the affliction of the afflicted; and he has not hid his face from him; he has heard when he cried to him. The afflicted shall feast and be satisfied. All the ends of the earth shall remember and turn to the Lord; and all the families of the nations shall worship before him. For dominion belongs to the Lord, and he rules over the nations. Yea, to him shall all the great of the earth bow down. Before him shall bow down all who go down to the dust. Posterity shall serve him; men shall tell of the Lord to the next generation, and proclaim his deliverance to a people yet unborn, that he has wrought it." Psalm 22.

It is so wonderful to know that Psalm 23 follows Psalm 22!

The triumph of the cross is celebrated. "The Lord is my Shepherd, I shall not want. He leads me in the footprints of righteousness to the waters of reflection where my soul remembers who I am! Even though I go through the valley of the shadow of death, I shall fear no evil!"

Then follows verse one of Psalm 24, "The earth is the Lord's and the fulness thereof; the world and those who dwell in it!"

Planet earth is God's property! A thief never becomes an owner! In all three the parables Jesus told in Luke 15, the word 'lost' as in lost sheep, lost coin and lost son, immediately implies ownership!

"He was wounded for our transgressions..." Is 53:4,5. Seven hundred years before it happens in our history, Isaiah sees the Plan of God; a mystery that none of the rulers of darkness understood. If they had insight into the mystery of God, they would never have crucified the Lord of glory. 1Cor.2:8-10.

Because of the law of the Incarnation, everything that happened to Jesus immediately represented and included the human race. Mankind is eternally associated in Christ. Ephesians 1:3,4. The word associate means: occurring together in close union, so as to co-here, in such a way that when any of them is afterwards presented to mind, the others are apt to be brought up in idea. This implies that it is impossible for God to entertain the thought of Jesus, and exclude man! In the mind of God, we are associated in Christ on equal terms!

1 Cor 1:30 Of God's doing are we in Christ. He is both the genesis and genius of our wisdom; a wisdom that reveals how righteous, sanctified and redeemed we already are in him. *(In God's economy, Christ represents us; what man could never achieve through personal discipline and willpower as taught in every religion, God's faith accomplished in Christ. Of his design are we in Christ; we are associated in oneness with him. Our wisdom is sourced in this union! Also our righteousness and holiness originate from him. Holiness = wholeness and harmony, spirit, soul and body. Our redemption is sanctioned*

in him. He redeemed our identity, our sanity, our health, our joy, our peace, our innocence and our complete well-being!)

"Therefore if any man be in Christ, he is a new creation. The old things have passed away. Behold, everything has become new!" 2 Cor 5:17

Notice that Paul did not say, "If any man is in Christ...", he said THERE-FORE if any man is in Christ!" The "therefore" changes the "if" from a condition to a conclusion! We are not "in Christ" through personal choice, "of God's doing are you in Christ" 1 Cor 1:30. God found us in Christ before he lost us in Adam!

2 Cor 5:14 The love of Christ [1]resonates within us and leaves us with only one conclusion: Jesus died humanity's death; therefore in God's logic every individual simultaneously died. (*[1]sunecho from sun, together with and echo, to echo, to embrace, to hold, thus translated, to resonate. Jesus didn't die 99% or for 99%. He died humanity's death one hundred percent! If Paul had to compromise the last part of verse 14 to read: "one died for all therefore only those who follow the prescriptions to qualify, have also died," then he would have had to change the first half of the verse as well! Only the love of Christ can make a calculation of such enormous proportion! Theology would question the extremity of God's love and perhaps prefer to add a condition or two to a statement like that!)* 2 Cor 5:15 Now if all were included in his death they were equally included in his resurrection. This unveiling of his love redefines human life! Whatever reference we could have of ourselves outside of our association with Christ is no longer relevant. 2 Cor 5:16 This is radical! No label that could possibly previously define someone carries any further significance! Even our pet doctrines of Christ are redefined. Whatever we knew about him historically or senti-mentally is challenged by this conclusion. *(By discovering Christ from God's point of view we discover ourselves and every other human life from God's point of view!)*

2 Cor 5:17 Now whoever you thought you were before, in Christ you are a brand new person! The old ways of seeing yourself and everyone else are over. Look! The resurrection of Jesus has made everything new! *(Just imagine this! Whoever a person was as a Jew, Greek, slave or freeman, Boer, Zulu, Xhosa, British, Indian, Moslem or American, Chinese, Japanese or Congolese; is now dead and gone! They all died when Jesus died! Remember we are not talking the law language here! The 'If' in, "If any man is in Christ" is not a condition, it is the almighty conclusion of the revelation of the gospel! Man is in Christ by God's doing. 1 Cor 1:30, Eph 1:4. 2 Cor 5:14-16 gives context to verse 17! For so long we studied verse 17 on its own and interpreted the 'if' as a condition! Paul did not say, "If any man is in Christ," he said "THEREFORE if any man is in Christ..." The therefore immediately includes verses 14 to 16! If God's faith sees every man in Christ in his death, then they were certainly also in Christ in his resurrection.*

Jesus did not reveal a 'potential' you, he revealed the truth about you so that you may know the truth about yourself and be free indeed!)

2 Cor 5:18 To now see everything as new is to simply see what God has always known in Christ; we are not debating man's experience, opinion, or his contribution; this is 100% God's belief and his doing. In Jesus Christ God [1]exchanged equivalent value to redeem us to himself; this act of reconciliation is the mandate of our ministry. *([1]katalasso, reconciliation; a mutual exchange of equal value.)*

2 Cor 5:19 Our ministry declares that Jesus did not act independent of God; Christ is proof that God reconciled the total kosmos to himself. Deity and humanity embraced in Christ; the fallen state of mankind was deleted; their trespasses would no longer count against them! God has placed this message within us; he now announces his friendship with every individual from within us!

2 Cor 5:20 The voice God has in Christ he now has in us; we are God's ambassadors; our lives exhibit the urgency of God to [1]persuade everyone to realize the reconciliation of their redeemed identity. *(Persuade, plead, [1]parakaleo, from para, a preposition indicating close proximity, a thing proceeding from a sphere of influence, with a suggestion of union of place of residence, to have sprung from its author and giver, originating from, denoting the point from which an action originates, intimate connection, and kaleo, to identify by name, to surname.*

See Luke 15:28,31, His father pleaded with him, "My child, you are always with me, and all that I have is yours."

"Be reconciled" could not be translated, "Become reconciled!" "Do in order to become" is the language of the Old Testament; the language of the New is, "Be, because of what was done!"

2 Cor 5:21 This is the divine exchange: he who knew no [1]sin embraced our distortion; he appeared to be without form; this was the mystery of God's prophetic [2]poetry; he was disguised in our distorted image; marred with our iniquities; he took our sorrows, our pain, our shame to his grave and birthed his righteousness in us. He took our sins and we became his innocence. *([1]hamartia, from ha, without and meros, form; [2]poema; we were born anew in his resurrection from the dead.)*

(Isa 52:10 The LORD has bared his holy arm before the eyes of all the nations, and all the ends of the earth shall see the salvation of our God. Isa 52:14 Just as many were astonished at you—so was he marred in his appearance, more than any human, and his form beyond that of human semblance— Isa 52:15 so will he

startle many nations. Kings will shut their mouths at him; for what had not been told them they will see, and what they had not heard they will understand. "Surely he has borne our griefs, and carried our sorrows; yet we esteemed him stricken, smitten of God, and afflicted. But surely he was wounded for our transgressions; he was bruised for our iniquities; the chastisement of our peace was on him; and with his stripes we ourselves are healed. Isaiah 53:4-5. The point is not how we esteemed him, but how he esteemed us!

Deut 32:5,6. They have corrupted themselves; they did not behave as his children, they have become a distorted generation of people, twisted out of their true pattern; they are a crooked and perverse generation. (Paul quotes this very verse in Phil 2:15.)

Deut 32:18 You were unmindful of the Rock that begot you and have forgotten the God who danced with you. (Hebrew, kgheel, to dance)

Rom 8:29 He pre-designed and engineered us from the start to be jointly fashioned in the same mold and image of his son according to the exact blueprint of his thought. We see the original and intended pattern of our lives preserved in his Son. He is the firstborn from the same womb that reveals our genesis. He confirms that we are the invention of God. (We were born anew when he was raised from the dead! 1 Pet 1:3. His resurrection co-reveals our common genesis. No wonder then that he is not ashamed to call us his brethren! We indeed share the same origin. Heb.2:11.) Rom 8:30 Jesus reveals that man pre-existed in God; he defines us. He justified us and also glorified us. He redeemed our innocence and restored the glory we lost in Adam. (Rom 3:23,24; prohoritso, pre defined, like when an architect draws up a detailed plan; kaleo, to surname, identify by name.

Titus 2:11 The grace of God shines as bright as day making the salvation of humankind undeniably visible.)

On the mountain of transfiguration, Moses no longer sees the Promise from afar; he looks into the eyes of God's Canaan. *(Math.17)* The Promised Land is no longer a geographical address on the planet, or a future expectation, but one New Incarnate Man that represents and embraces the entire human race! See 2 Cor 1:18-20 God's certainty is our persuasion; there is no maybe in him!

The son of God, Jesus Christ whom I, Paul, Sylvanus and Timothy boldly announced in you is God's ultimate yes to mankind; human life is associated in all that he is. In God's mind there exists not even a hint of hesitation about this! In him the detail of every single promise of God is fulfilled; Jesus is God's yes to your total well being! In our union with him the Amen that echoes in us gives evidence to his glorious intent through us.

The Sabbath, even in its prophetic shadow has always been a celebration of perfection! "On the Sabbath you shall do no work!" The Sabbath is no longer a shadow-day in the Jewish week but a living Person! Jesus fulfilled everything that God's faith celebrated since the first Sabbath! He redeemed the image and likeness of God in human form.

Col 2:16 Do not let anyone therefore bring a restriction to your freedom by reviving religious rules and regulations pertaining to eating and drinking; all Jewish festivals, new moons and Sabbaths have come to an end in Christ! *(Their relevance only served to remind of the promise of Christ on an annual, monthly and weekly basis. They carried the promise like a placenta would hold the unborn child, but became obsolete as soon as the child was born.)* Col 2:17 These things were only prophetic shadows; Christ is the substance. The complete dispensation of the law and the prophets is represented in Moses and Elijah. They foresaw this moment and proclaimed its implication.

Luk 24:27 And beginning at Moses and all the prophets, he expounded unto them in all the scriptures the things concerning himself. Luk 24:44,45 And he said unto them, These are the words which I spake unto you, while I was yet with you, that all things must be fulfilled, which were written in the law of Moses, and in the prophets, and in the psalms, concerning me. Then opened he their understanding, that they might understand the scriptures,

Heb 1:1 Throughout ancient times God spoke in many fragments and glimpses of prophetic thought to our fathers.

Heb 1:2 Now, the sum total of his conversation with man has finally culminated in a son. He is the official heir of all things. He is, after all, the author of the ages. Jesus is what has been on the tip of the Father's tongue all along! *(The revelation of man's redeemed sonship, as revealed in Jesus, is the crescendo of God's conversation with humanity. Throughout the ages he has whispered his name in disguise to be revealed in the fullness of time as the greatest surprise.*

The exact image of God his very likeness, the authentic eternal thought became voice and was made flesh in us. The composer of a concert masterpiece knew that the notes scribbled on a page, would finally find its voice in a symphony of instruments.)

Heb 1:3 We have our beginning and our being in him. He is the force of the universe, sustaining everything that exists by his eternal utterance! Jesus is the radiant and flawless expression of the person of God. He makes the glory *(doxa, intent)* of God visible and exemplifies the character and every attribute of God in human form. *(Gen.1:26, 27)* This powerful final utterance of God *(the incarnation revealing our sonship)* is the vehicle that carries the weight of the universe. What he communicates is the central theme of everything that exists. The content of his message celebrates the fact that God took it upon himself to successfully cleanse and acquit humankind. The man Jesus is now his right hand of power, the executive authority seated in the boundless measure of his majesty. He occupies the highest seat of dominion to endorse our innocence! His throne is established upon our innocence. *("Having accomplished purification of sins, he sat down...")*

This Word that became flesh is the culmination of God's thought; sonship accurately articulates the heartbeat of God. Imagine God finding a word, worthy to hold his ultimate thought; his final, eternal most intimate word to mankind. He frames this word not in an ancient language of men or angels, but in an earthen jar, a clay pot, Jesus, the last Adam, the New Man, at the same time the mirror radiance of the fullness of God in you! The incarnation is God's language.

2 Cor 3:2 Instead of an impressive certificate framed on my wall I have you framed in my heart! You are our epistle written within us! You are an open letter; you speak a global language; one that everyone can [1]read and recognize as their mother tongue! *([1]anaginosko, to know again, recognize, to read with recognition.)* 3:3 The fact that you are a Christ-Epistle shines as bright as day! This is what our ministry is all about. The Spirit of God is the living ink. Every trace of the Spirit's influence on the heart is what gives permanence to this conversation. We are not talking law-language here; this is more dynamic and permanent than letters chiseled in stone; this conversation is embroidered in your inner consciousness. *(It is the life of your design that grace echoes within you!)*

Truth finds its most authentic and articulate expression in human life; this beats any doctrinal debate!

God spoke everything into existence, but having created man in his image and likeness, he now fashions a body of clay with his hands from the dust of the earth. "O Lord, you are our Father, we are the clay and you are the potter; we all are the work of your hand!" Isaiah 64:8. You are hand crafted by God; designed by his touch, for touch.

In 1947 a Bedouin shepherd-boy discovers the Qumran-scrolls in clay pots in a cave! These scrolls proved to be the most ancient and authentic text to confirm the historic integrity of Isaiah and many of the other books of the Bible. More than 800 scrolls represent a library of scriptures hidden away in caves near Qumran around the outbreak of the Jewish-Roman war in 66A.D. The library belonged to a group called the Essenes who were led by a priest they called 'The Teacher of Righteousness'. Today, the most accurate and authentic Word, the display of the Presence and Person of God, is his life preserved and revealed also in a clay pot, the human body, the incarnation. 2 Cor.4:7.

Many years after the transfiguration on the mountain Peter writes: "Concerning this salvation, the prophets who spoke of the grace that was to be yours, searched diligently to find out the exact time and circumstances to which the Spirit of the Messiah within them was pointing when they predicted the sufferings of Christ and the subsequent glorious implication thereof. It was revealed to them that they were not serving their own generation but you, when they spoke of the things that have now been announced to you by those who have preached the gospel to you by the Holy Spirit... therefore gird up your minds to embrace the full intent of God." 1 Pet 1: 10-12. The hour has come for the son of man to be glorified...the single grain of wheat died and did not abide alone. John 12:23,24.

1 Cor 2:2 The testimony of God is my only persuasion concerning you: Jesus Christ died your death on the cross! I can see you in no other light! 1 Cor 2:7 We whisper words of wisdom, hidden in silence for timeless ages; the mystery which God had planned with accurate precision: the glory that we had lost in Adam are restored again in Christ! *(God found us in Christ, before he lost us in Adam!)* 1 Cor 2:8 Neither the politicians nor the theologians of the day had a clue about this mystery *(of mankind's association in Christ);* if they did, they would never have crucified the Lord whose death redeemed our glory! Mirror Bible.

God's work of redemption is valid with immediate effect. "We have received a faith of equal standing. His divine power granted to us all things that pertain to life and godliness through the knowledge of him." 2 Peter 1:1,3.

Peter wishes for every believer to have a first-hand encounter with Jesus, to know him for who he really is and not just as a vague, distant, historic figure. He writes that he was not relating cleverly devised myths, but was an eyewitness of the majesty of Jesus; he saw his body transformed into light and he heard the voice that day on the mountain, "this is my beloved Son with whom I am well pleased." Now the prophetic word is confirmed beyond doubt. We can argue, "Well that is great for Peter; he was one of the lucky ones to be an eyewitness. What about us?" This is exactly what prompted Peter to write this letter. "You will do well to pay attention to the prophetic word and to my testimony as to a lamp shining in a dark place until the day dawns and the morning star rises in your own hearts!" See the Mirror Bible, 2 Pet.1:17 "He was spectacularly endorsed by God the Father in the highest honor and glory.

God's majestic voice announced, "This is the son of my delight, he has my total approval." 2 Pet 1:18 For John, James and I the prophetic word is fulfilled beyond doubt; we heard this voice loud and clear from the heavenly realm while we were with Jesus in that sacred moment on the mountain. 1:19 For us the appearing of the Messiah is no longer a future promise, but a fulfilled reality; now it's your turn to have more than a second hand, hear-say testimony, take my word as one would take a lamp at night, the day is about to dawn for you in your own understanding; when the morning star appears, you no longer need the lamp, this will happen shortly on the horizon of your own hearts."

The reading of the Bible and spiritual literature serves merely as a lamp, a catalyst to awaken the revelation of Christ in you. It is impossible to cook a meal in the heat of a single match; but the match is enough to light the oven!

A young man of noble birth Saul, who excels in zeal for the tradition of his religion, is more ambitious and recognised than any of his contemporaries, pursues his mission to wipe out the followers and influence of this Jesus. Suddenly a light brighter than the sun overwhelms him; he is blinded for three days, but he has Christ revealed within him.

2 Cor 4:6 The light source is founded in the same God who said, "Light, be!" And light shone out of darkness! He lit the lamp in our understanding so that we may clearly recognize the features of his likeness in the face of Jesus Christ reflected within us. (*The same God who bade light shine out of darkness has kindled a light in our hearts, whose shining is to make known his glory as he has revealed it in the features of Jesus Christ. Knox*)

2 Cor 4:7 We have discovered this treasure where it was hidden all along, in these frail skin-suits made of clay. We take no credit for finding it there! It took the enormous power of God in the achievement of Christ to rescue our minds from the lies it believed. (*See Math 13:44 "The kingdom of heaven is like treasure hidden in an agricultural field, which a man found and covered up; then in his joy he goes and sells all that he has and buys that field. God invested all that he has in the redeeming of our original value! He rescued the life of our design. Our inner life hosts the treasure of the life of our design; Jesus said in John 7:37,38, If you believe that I am what the scriptures are all about, you will know that you are what I am all about and rivers of living water will gush out of your innermost being!*)

This is Paul's "repentance", his metanoia moment! The Greek word translated "repentance" is the word metanoia, from meta, together with, and nous, mind; this word suggests a complete mind shift; from now on therefore Paul no longer knows himself after the flesh; in fact he now no longer knows any one from a human point of view. 2 Cor 5:16, Isa 55:8-11. To discover how mindful God is of us ignites metanoaia! Jesus is God's mind made up about "you-manity"!

In a moment Paul understands the mystery of the gospel! Jesus represents the human race.

The danger was never to exaggerate such a great salvation! It was always in underestimating it! In 1 Cor 2:9 Paul quotes Isa 64:4, It is written: "What has been concealed for ages in a realm inaccessible to the senses; what no human eye could catch a glimpse of, nor man's ear could even hear a whisper of, neither could the inquiring mind decipher the code of that mystery which God has already [1]fully arranged and was ready to reveal to [2]those who love him." *(The exact detail of his plan to rescue his image and likeness in man was in place. How Jesus would represent humanity to die their death was the wisdom of God concealed. In the mind of God we were associated in Christ before the ages; this was according to God's eternal resolve. "The things that God has prepared," [1]hetoimatzo, from the oriental custom of sending on before kings on their journeys persons to level the roads and make them passable. What seemed a cul-de-sac for the flesh is a royal highway for faith. The redemption of man was not to be the product of human philosophy or speculation. In Isa 64:4 the Hebrew word [2]ghaka, to carve an image; to show by drawing or description, piercing, is the word translated, those who 'wait upon the Lord'. Paul writes in Greek when he quotes Isaiah and uses the phrase, "for those who love him." Thus faith opens the horizon of love's mystery; it is a place where thoughts carve an impression; a place not accessible to the scrutiny of a suspicious academic or religious guilt and performance based approach. See 1 Cor 3:20.)*

One has died for all! There is no longer Jew or Gentile, not even male or female, slave or freeman, but one new man! Gal 3:28 Nothing resembles your previous identity as Jew or Gentile, bond or free, male or female, Billabong or Gucci. In Christ each one of you are equally significant. In the mind of God, every Jew and every Gentile died the moment Jesus died. One has died for all therefore all have died! 2 Cor.5:14.

Eph 2:11 Remember where you came from; (not only were you spiritually dead but) it wasn't long ago when you were still classified as non-Jewish, judging on the surface you had nothing that linked you to them. They sneered at you because you didn't share their distinguishing mark of circumcision, which was their claim to fame!

Eph 2:12 During that time you were distanced from the Messianic hope; you had nothing in common with Israel; you felt foreign to the covenants of prophetic promise, living a life with nothing to look forward to in a world where God seemed absent.

Eph 2:13 But now, wow! Everything has changed; you have discovered yourselves to be located in Christ. What once seemed so distant is now so near; his blood reveals your redeemed innocence and authentic genesis.

Eph 2:14 It is in him that we are one and at peace with everyone; he dissolved every definition of division.

Eph 2:15 In his incarnation, he rendered the entire Jewish system of ceremonial laws and regulations useless as a measure to justify human life and conduct. In that he died humanity's death all ground for tension and hostility was entirely removed. The peace he proclaims reveals one new human race, created and defined in Christ, instead of two groups of people separated by their ethnic identity and differences.

Eph 2:16 Both parties are fully represented and reconciled to God in one human body through the cross. He reinstated the former harmony; all opposing elements were thus utterly defeated.

Eph 2:17 On that basis he made his public appearance, proclaiming the good news of peace to universal mankind; both those who felt left out in the cold, (as far as the promises and covenants were concerned,) as well as to those who were near all along, (because of their Jewish identity.)

Eph 2:18 Because of Christ both Jew and Gentile now enjoy equal access to the Father in one Spirit.

Eph 2:19 The conclusion is clear, you are no longer frowned upon as a foreigner; you are where you belong and part of an intimate family where no-one is suspicious or inferior.

This revelation becomes the passion of Paul's new mission: to reveal Christ in every man. His mandate is to make all men see! Eph.3:9, Col 1:28.

Gal 1:16 This is the heart of the gospel that I proclaim; it began with an unveiling of sonship [1]in me, freeing me to announce the same sonship [2]in the masses of non-Jewish people. I felt no immediate urgency to compare notes with those who were familiar with Christ from a mere historic point of view. *(The Greek text is quite clear, "It pleased the Father to reveal his son in me in order that I may proclaim him in the nations!" [1]en emoi, in me, and [2]en ethnos, in the Gentile nations, or the masses of non Jewish people! Not 'among' the Gentiles as most translations have it. Later when Barnabas is sent to investigate the conversion of the Greeks in Acts 11, instead of reporting his findings to the HQ in Jerusalem, he immediately finds Paul, knowing that Paul's gospel is the revelation of the mystery of Christ in the nations. Col.1:27. No wonder then that those believers were the first to be called Christians, or Christ-like!*

Jesus Christ confirms that the son of man is the son of God. Mat 23:9 "Call no man your father on earth, for you have one Father, who is in heaven." Paul reminds the Greek philosophers in Acts 17 that we live and move and have our being in God; humankind is indeed the offspring of God. He is quoting from their own writings, Aratus, who lived 300 BC. The incorruptible seed of sonship is as much in every man as the seed is already in all soil, even in the desert, waiting for the rain to awaken and ignite its life!

"For as the rain and the snow come down from heaven and water the earth, making it bring forth and sprout, so shall my word be that proceeds from my mouth, it shall not disappoint my purpose, it shall saturate the soil and cause it to bring forth and sprout, instead of the thorn the cyprus and instead of the brier the myrtle!" Is 55:8-11,13.

In Math. 13:44 Jesus says that the kingdom of heaven is like a treasure hidden in an agricultural field! There is more to the field than what meets the eye! In 2 Cor 4:4 and 7 Paul says that we have this treasure in earthen vessels! But the god of this world seeks to blind our minds through unbelief (believing a lie about ourselves, Num13:33) to keep us from seeing the light of the gospel revealing the glory of God in the face of Christ who is the image of God, as in a mirror!

When Jesus speaks of the sinner he speaks of him as the lost sheep, coin, or son. Lk.15. The inscription and image did not disappear from the coin when it was lost, how can we praise God and with the same mouth curse a man made in his image? James 3:9, Luke 20:20-26. Mankind forgot what manner of man he is by design; man is the image and likeness bearer of his Maker; this is exactly what Jesus came to reveal and redeem.

We may now behold him with unveiled faces as in a mirror and be immediately transformed (in our understanding) into his likeness. From the glory (opinion) of the flesh to the glory (opinion) of God. Legalistic religion kept the veil in place; the proclaiming of the liberating truth of the Good News, removes the veil! The 'ugly duckling' didn't need a facelift or lessons on how to fake the swan life! It only needed to know the truth about itself to be free indeed.)

Gal 1:17   This is radical! I deliberately distanced myself from Jerusalem and the disciples of Jesus. I landed up in Arabia before I returned again to Damascus. *(The weight of this revelation left me no choice; instead of finding out more about Christ in history, I desire to discover him more in me! See also 2 Cor.5:16)*

Gal 1:18   Then three years later I ventured into Jerusalem, specifically to meet with [1]Kefas; I ended up staying with him for two weeks. *([1]Aramaic for rock, kefas, Greek for rock, petros,. Paul here calls him Kefas in order to emphasize the meaning of his name rather than the familiar sound of Peter. Jesus said that the revelation of man's true identity and origin is the rock foundation of the ekklesia,*

71

lit. original identity from ek, preposition denoting origin and kaleo, to surname. Mat.16:13- 18. See also Isa.51:1 and Deut. 32:18, 1 Peter 2:5, 1 Kings 6:7.)

Gal 1:19 During this time I did not see any of the other apostles except James, the younger brother of Jesus. *(Saul (Paul), Peter (Kefas) and James shared a vital revelation, all three of them discovered their original identity beyond their natural birth, "Simon son of Jonah, flesh and blood did not reveal to you that I, the son of man am the Christ, the son of God; now that you know who I am, allow me to introduce you to you! I say that you are Rock. Math.16:17,18.*

During the three years of Jesus' ministry none of his brothers believed in him. John 7:5, but in 1 Cor.15:7 Paul specifically mention the fact that Jesus also appeared to James after his resurrection. Suddenly it dawns on James that the Father of lights birthed mankind by the eternal Word of truth, the word that became flesh and died humanity's death and who co-raised humankind into newness of life in his resurrection. If any man hears this word he sees the face of his birth as in a mirror! As Peter later admitted "We were born anew when Jesus was raised from the dead!" 1 Pet 1:3.The word that was before time was is our genesis. James 1:17,18, 23,24.)

"I have made you a light to the nations that you may bring salvation to the ends of the earth." Acts 13:47. "All flesh shall see the glory of the Lord." Is.40:5.

Rom.8:19 "Our lives now represent the one event every creature anticipates with held breath, standing on tip-toe as it were to witness the unveiling of the sons of God. Can you hear the drum-roll?" Mirror Bible.

"Arise and shine, for your light has come and the glory of the Lord is risen upon you! Kings and nations shall come to the brightness of your rising!" Isaiah 60:1-3.

The coming of Jesus forever divided human history into a before and after Christ- calendar. Jesus is the completeness of time; he gives context and relevance to the life of our design. Every prophetic promise concludes in him.

Paul's writing to the Galatians prompts them to make the transition in their minds from the shadow system of the law to the substance of the grace life. It is time!

Gal 4:1 An infant heir has no more say than a slave, even though he owns everything! *(The best deal the law could possibly broker confirmed man's slavery to sin.)* Gal 4:2 He would remain under domestic supervision and house rules until the date fixed by his father for his official graduation to the status of sonship. Gal 4:3 This is exactly how it was with us; we were kidnapped as it were into infancy and confined to that state through the law. *(An inferior mindset as a result of Adam's fall.)*

Gal 4:4 But then the day dawned; the most complete culmination of time! *(Everything predicted was concluded in Christ!)* The son arrived, commissioned by the Father; his legal passport to the planet was his mother's womb. In a human body exactly like ours he lived his life subject to the same scrutiny of the law.

Gal 4:5 His mandate was to rescue the human race from the regime of the law of performance and announce the revelation of their true sonship in God. *(Now our true state of sonship is again realized! John 1:12. See: John 1:11-14 "It was not as though he arrived on a foreign planet, he came to his own, yet his own did not recognize him Ps.24:1. But to everyone who realizes their association in him, convinced that he is their original life, in them he confirms that we are his offspring. These are they who discover their genesis in God beyond their natural conception! Man began in God. We are not the invention of our parents! Suddenly the invisible eternal Word takes on visible form! The Incarnation! In him, in us! The most accurate tangible display of God's eternal thought finds expression in human life! The Word became a human being; we are his address; he resides in us! He captivates our gaze! The glory we see there is not a religious replica; he is the authentic **monogenes** begotten only of God. In him we recognize our true beginning. The Glory that Adam lost, returns! In fullness! Only Grace can communicate truth in such complete context!)*

Gal 4:6 To seal our sonship God has commissioned the Spirit of sonship to resonate the Abba echo in our hearts; and now, in our innermost being we recognize him as our true and very dear Father. *(Rom. 8:14 The original life of the Father revealed in his son is the life the Spirit now conducts within us. 8:15 Slavery is such a poor substitute for sonship! They are opposites; the one leads forcefully through fear; sonship responds fondly to Abba Father. 8:16 His Spirit resonates within our spirit to confirm the fact that we originate in God. 8:17 Because we are his offspring, we qualify to be his heirs, God himself is our portion, we co-inherit with Christ.)*

Gal 4:7 Can you see how foolish it would be for a son to continue to live his life with a slave mentality? Your sonship qualifies you to immediately participate in all the wealth of God's inheritance which is yours because of Christ. *(Legalism in its every disguise contradicts sonship! Sonship is not for sale!)*

Gal 4:8 What really amazes me is how gullible you gentile believers are to get yourselves all tangled up again in oppressive Jewish rites! I mean you know all about your BC days of slavery to imaginary gods under your pagan beliefs. Gal 4:9 In the mean time you have come to know the real God, *(quite unlike the god of your imagination)*; what is most significant however, is to discover that he knew you all along! After all this, how could you possibly feel attracted again to the pathetic principles of religious deception? It does not matter in what disguise legalism comes, whether pagan or Jewish, it brings the same bondage. Gal 4:10 All of a sudden there are special days, months, seasonal and annual festivities that are scrupulously celebrated; this is nothing more than superstitious religious sentiment.

Gal 4:22 The law records the fact that Abraham had two sons: one by a slave girl, the other by a free woman. Gal 4:23 The one is produced by the flesh *(the DIY-tree)*, the other by faith *(the promise)*. Gal 4:24 There is a parallel meaning in the story of the two sons: they represent two systems, works and grace.

Gal 4:25 Sinai is an Arabian rocky mountain named after Hagar, *(outside the land of promise)*. Its association with the law of Moses mirrors Jerusalem as the capital of Jewish legalism. Hager is the mother of the law of works.

Gal 4:26 But the mother from above, the true mother of mankind is grace, the free Jerusalem; she is the mother of the promise.

Gal 4:27 For it is written, "Rejoice o childless one! Erupt in jubilee! For though you have never known travail before, your children will greatly outnumber her who was married *(to the law)*.

Gal 4:28 We resemble Isaac: we are begotten of faith, the promise is our parent.

Gal 4:29 Just as when the flesh child persecuted the faith child, so now these Jerusalem Jews in their Christian disguise seek to harass you;

Gal 4:30 however, scripture is clear: "Expel the slave mother and her son; the slave son cannot inherit with the free son." *(In exactly the same way, rid your minds radically from the slave mother and child mentality.)*

Gal 4:31 Realize whose children we are my brothers: we are not sons of the slave-mother, the law, but sons of the free mother; we are sons of grace!

Gal 5:1 Christ defines your faith; he is your freedom from anything the law could never free you from! Find your firm footing in this freedom. Do not let religion trip you up again and harness you to a system of rules and obligations! *(In this parallel, Christ represents Sarah, the faith-mother who birthed you in the resurrection. The rock-hewn tomb represents Sarah's dead womb! 1 Pet.1:3)*

Eph 4:8 Scripture confirms that he led us as trophies in his triumphant procession on high; he [1]repossessed his gift *(likeness)* in man. *(See Ephesians 2:6, We are also elevated in his ascension to be equally welcome in the throne room of the heavenly realm where we are now seated together with him in his authority. Quote from the Hebrew text, Ps 68:18, [1]lakachta mattanoth baadam, thou hast taken gifts in man, in Adam. [The gifts which Jesus Christ distributes to man he has received in man, in and by virtue of his incarnation. Commentary by Adam Clarke.]*

God is not watching us from a distance, as the song suggests. Emmanuel means God with us. God can never again be God without us! God cannot get any closer to mankind than what he already did in the person of Jesus! He is not nearer to some than what he is to others, nor nearer to Jerusalem than to Japan. As much as Jesus represents all of God, he represents the entire human race in one person.

Imagine God finding a word, worthy to hold his ultimate thought; his final, eternal most intimate word to mankind. He frames this word not in an ancient language of men or angels, but in an earthen jar, a clay pot, Jesus, the last Adam, the New Man, at the same time the mirror radiance of the fullness of God in you!

God has found a face in you that portrays him more beautifully than the best theo-logy! Your features, your touch, the cadence of your voice, the compassion in your gaze, the lines in your smile, the warmth of your person and presence unveils him!

We sometimes get the idea that God speaks in very exclusive and economic ways; we think that his words are rare and have even developed organisations, called "church" where we pay a priest or a pastor to hear God on our behalf.

But in fact, you do not even have to wait for next Sunday! "Wisdom cries aloud in the street; in the market-places she raises her voice; on the top of the walls she cries out; at the entrance of the city gates she speaks; "How long, O simple ones, will you love being simple? How long will scoffers delight in their scoffing, and fools hate knowledge? Turn to me, and I will pour out my thoughts to you! I will make my words known to you!" Proverbs 1:20-23.

If man's design and inner make-up is such, that we are to be sustained by the word that proceeds from of the mouth of God, then his word must be more readily available than our daily, freshly baked bread! "Man shall not live by bread alone, but by every word that proceeds from the mouth of God." Deut.8:3.

The word translated, 'every', is the Hebrew word, kol, which means complete. The Word in its most complete form is not the book but the message spoken in the Person of Jesus Christ. He is John 1:1 and 14. The most accurate translation is the Incarnation!

Joh 5:39 "You have your heads in your Bibles constantly because you think you'll find eternal life there. But you miss the forest for the trees. These Scriptures are all about me!" The Message

Many doctrines of men are based on isolated scripture references outside of the context of God's work of redemption as it is revealed in Christ. Any concept that excludes the good news of what God achieved on humanity's behalf in Christ is irrelevant, no matter how many scriptures can be quoted. Jesus as the revealer and Redeemer of God's blueprint image and likeness in human form is the context of scripture. Not even the historic or traditional setting of Scripture can distract from the revelation of Christ in man. Luke 24:27,44.

Reading the Old Covenant without understanding that Christ is the fulfilment of Scripture is a complete waste of time. 2 Cor 3:14; Luk 24:27,44,45.

Hear David's song in Psalm 19,
"The heavens are telling the glory of God;
the firmament proclaims his handiwork.
Day to day pours forth speech,

and night-to-night declares knowledge.
There is no speech; nor are there words;
Their voice is not heard, yet their range (or resonance) goes out through all the earth. *(Resonance, Hebrew: kawa –to intertwine, to bind together by twisting, a musical string or accord, a measuring line; same word also used in Isa.40, they that kawa with God renew their strength.)*
Their words reach the ends of the world.
In them he has set a tent for the Sun,
which comes forth like a Bridegroom leaving his chamber,
and like a strong man runs its course with joy;
its rising is from the end of the heavens,
and its circuit to the end of them;
and there is nothing hid from its heat.
The law of the Lord is perfect *(the perfect law of liberty)*
reviving the soul;
the testimony of the Lord is sure,
making wise the simple;
the precepts of the Lord are right;
rejoicing the heart;
the word of the Lord is pure,
enlightening the eyes;
more to be desired are they than gold,
even much fine gold;
sweeter also than honey,
and drippings of the honey comb.
The words of my mouth and the meditation of my heart,
now mirror yours, O Lord, my Rock and my Redeemer"

Rom 1:18 Mankind foolishly [1]suppressed and concealed the truth in their unrighteousness; *(The word [1]katecho, to echo downwards is the opposite to anoche, to echo upwards, see Rom 2:4 and Rom 3:26. See Col 2:2,3. The law reveals how guilty and sinful man is, while the gospel reveals how forgiven and restored to his original blueprint man is.)*

Rom 1:19 even though God is not a stranger to anyone, for what can be known of God is already manifest in them. *(The law reveals how guilty and sinful man is, while the gospel reveals how forgiven and restored to his original blueprint man is.)*

Rom 1:20 God is on display in creation; the very fabric of visible cosmos appeals to reason. It clearly bears witness to the ever present sustaining power and intelligence of the invisible God, leaving man without any valid excuse to ignore him. *(Ps.19:1 God's glory is on tour in the skies, God-craft on exhibit across the horizon. :2 Madame Day holds classes every morning, Professor Night lectures each evening. :3 Their words aren't heard, their voices aren't recorded, :4 But their silence fills the earth: unspoken truth is spoken everywhere. The Message)*

Rom 1:21 Yet man only knew him in a philosophical religious way, from a distance, and failed to give him credit as God. Their taking him for granted and lack of gratitude veiled him from them; they became absorbed in useless debates and discussions, which further darkened their understanding about themselves.rom Rom 1:22 Their wise conclusions only proved folly. Rom 1:23 Their losing sight of God, made them lose sight of who they really were. In their calculation the image and likeness of God became reduced to a corrupted and distorted pattern of themselves. Suddenly man has more in common with the creepy crawlies than with his original blueprint. Rom 1:24 It seemed like God abandoned mankind to be swept along by the lusts of their own hearts to abuse and defile themselves. *(Their most personal possession, their own bodies, became worthless public property.)* Rom 1:25 Instead of embracing their Maker as their true identity they preferred the deception of a warped identity, religiously giving it their affection and devotion. Rom 1:26 By being confused about their Maker they became confused about themselves.

In Isa 55:8-11 God exposes and solves the heart of mankind's problem; there is nothing wrong with the human race, because there is nothing wrong with their design or their redemption! There is only something horribly wrong with their thinking! "Your thoughts are not my thoughts; therefore your ways are not my ways! As the heavens are higher than the earth, so are my thoughts higher than your thoughts, and my ways higher than your ways..."

We often stop reading there and then use this scripture as a reference to explain why we do not understand the ways of God; yet the very next verse pulsates with good news! Picture a farmer looking with urgent expectation at the promise of rain in the clouds; knowing that the water his crops so desparately need could be on its way! But how does the farmer connect the promise in the sky with his field? Religion offers a multitude of self-help plans and recipies to build extension ladders into the heavens and engineer a prayer-pipeline! Prayer-plumbing, they should call it! Every possible sincere effort to persuade a reluctant god to help, is employed! Religion needs paying and returning customers, and thrives on two lies: distance and delay! Jesus cancelled both those illusions! The hour has come! Every possible definition of distance is cancelled! "But as sure as the rain and the snow come down from heaven and water the earth, saturates the soil and awakens the seed, making it bring forth and sprout, giving seed to the sower and bread for food, so shall my word be that proceeds from my mouth, says God." Jesus is the word that proceeded out of the Father's mouth! The prophetic word is the rain that saturated the earth and brought forth the incarnation! Eph 1:3, Let's celebrate God! He lavished every blessing heaven has upon us in Christ! The incarnation is the fulfilment of Isa 55:10,11! The word was always destined to become flesh and tabernacle within us!

Mankind is not designed to live by bread alone; but by every word that proceeds from the mouth of God! The mouth of God is the source of the authentic word, Deut 8:3. The term, 'mouth of God' places the emphasis on the source; the eye of the fountain. Not the diluted opinion of human tradition and interpretation.

The outcome is predictable! Both the seed and the soil understand the language of the rain. The incarnation mirrors and awakens the incorruptible seed within you and is destined to accomplish the eternal purpose of God. The soil of the earth, the flesh of man shall again unveil the image and likeness of God. The taberancle of God is within you! The Incarnation forever bridges every distance that could possibly separate man from God. God is in our face! His word has become flesh!

"The people who dwelt in darkness have seen a great light" Mathew 4:16. "The true light that enlightens every man has come into the world." John 1:1-5,9,14,16.

"You are the light of the world, like a city set on a hill, its light cannot be hid." Mathew 5:14. "Let your light so shine, that men will see your good works and glorify the Father." The Greek word for glorify or glory is the word, doxa, it means opinion. When people encounter what God does through you, they discover the opinion of God about them! Matthew 5:16. "Arise and shine, for your light has come, and the glory of the Lord is risen upon you. Behold, darkness shall cover the earth, and thick darkness, the people. But the glory of the Lord will arise upon you, and his glory will be seen upon you. And the nations shall come to your light, and kings to the brightness of your rising." Isaiah 60:1-3.

Talking about living an irresistibly attractive life! God endeavors to accomplish his will in the world through you. You do not have to ask God what his plan is for your life; your life is his plan!

Hearing that every good and perfect gift comes from above, from the Father of lights, who brought us forth by the word of truth, is like seeing the face of your birth, your inner-self as you really are, as in a mirror. James 1:17,18.

We are his perfect gift to one another. Eph 4:11 What God now has in us is gift wrapped to the world; we are spirit; we are born from above; our outward appearance in the flesh seems a fragile vessel of clay, yet it holds an immortal treasure. The vessel takes its value from the treasure it holds. The value of the clay pot does not lie in its shape, size or colour. You can gym-trim your body and decorate your face and features with fancy make-up and expensive clothing and jewellery, but 'it's not on top, it's inside!' The cosmetic value of the clay pot can never compete with the treasure it holds. 2 Cor 4:7

Like the watermark on a paper note, our inner man carries the exact imprint of God's character and likeness. "The son radiates the glory of God and bears the very stamp of his nature." Heb 1: 3. We all have one origin. That is why Jesus is not ashamed to call us brethren. Hebrews 2:11. "He made from one, all of mankind. He is not far from each one of us, we are indeed his offspring." Acts 17:26-28. This 'watermark' parallel is also reflected in the seed concept. Every seed bears the exact genetic ingredient of the species. What ignites the life cycle and visible expression of the species is what matters most.

 The fountain within us is released when we discover the truth about us as it is revealed in Christ. He confirms that our basic design and make-up originate from the same thought.

In the core of our DNA and spirit being our original design reveals that God is mankind's author; we are his idea! We are his offspring!

To know the truth about every person adds a value to the individual that exceeds any talent, skill or achievement, or disappointment for that matter. Discovering the wealth within is what liberates and empowers one to be an asset and not a liability. This alone will break the bonds of poverty, greed and corruption. The compulsion to take and have is replaced with a desire to share and be useful out of the abundance of your being.

Eph 4:23 Pondering the incarnation, the truth about you displayed in Christ, will cause you to be completely reprogrammed in the way you think about yourself! *(This happens in the spirit of your mind, on a much deeper level than a mere intellectual and academic consent.)* Eph 4:28 If you were a thief before, you are one no more. Find an honest job where the fruit of your labour can be a blessing to others!

We often think that faith is to believe things we do not understand. Blind faith is an illusion; faith sees. This is why Paul says that faith comes to you in the revelation of Christ. Rom 10:17 "It is clear then that faith's source is found in the content of the message heard; the message is Christ. *(We are God's audience; Jesus is God's language; Jesus is what God believes about us! Greek, ek, a preposition that denotes source or origin, thus faith comes out of the word that reveals Christ. The word of "Christ" appears in the best manuscripts. See Rom 1:17 Herein lies the secret of the power of the gospel; there is no good news in it until the righteousness of God is revealed! [The good news is the fact that the cross of Christ was a success. God rescued the life of our design; he redeemed our innocence. Man would never again be judged righteous or unrighteous by his own ability to obey moral laws! It is not about what man must or must not do, but about what Jesus has done!] God now persuades everyone to believe what he knows to be true about them. [It is from faith to faith] The prophets wrote in advance about the fact that God believes that righteousness unveils the life that he always had in mind for us. "Righteousness by his [God's] faith defines life." Hab 2:4)* The broody hen counts her chickens before they are hatched; she already sees them in the shell.

These things are the most exciting truths your mind could ever ponder: understanding who you are in your union with God and your oneness with humanity; discovering your redeemed innocence and your individual uniqueness are the most noble thoughts you could possibly entertain. Falling head over heels in love with life is to love and admire God, your fellow man and yourself with equal esteem.

Jas 2:8 Scripture confirms that the law of the kingdom is fulfilled in you realizing the same value in your neighbor as you would see in yourself; this is what doing the word is all about, and it makes beautiful poetry. *(Lev 19:18; Lk 10:27, Mt 22:37-40. By not forgetting what manner of man you are, you will not forget what manner of man your neighbor is according to the mirror principle.)* Jas 2:12 Let the law of liberty set the pace *(be the judge)* in your conversation and conduct. *(The law of perfect liberty is the image and likeness of God revealed in Christ, now redeemed in man as in a mirror. Look deep enough into that law of faith that you may see there in its perfection a portrait that so resembles the original that he becomes distinctly visible in the spirit of your mind and in the face of every man you behold. Js 1:25)* Under the law of works and performance, which was often motivated by a sense of duty-, or even guilt-driven, this has always been impossible to achieve.

Jas 3:9 How can we can say beautiful things about God the Father but with the same mouth curse a man made in his mirror likeness? Jas 3:10 My brothers, a blessing and a curse ought not to originate from the same source.

Rom 12:10 Take tender care of one another with fondness and affection; esteem one another's unique value.

Rom 13:8 Remain debt free, the only thing we owe the world is our love. This is the essence of the law. Rom 13:9 Love makes it impossible for you to commit adultery, or to kill someone, or to steal from someone, speak evil of anyone, or to covet anything that belongs to someone else. Your only option is to esteem a fellow human with equal value to yourself.

Rom 13:10 Everything love does is to the advantage of another; therefore love is the most complete expression of what the law requires.

The mirror reveals our oneness. Paul says that while we compete with one another and strive for recognition, and measure and compare ourselves with one another, we are like people without understanding. 2 Corinthians 10:12. The only valid competition in the New Testament is to outdo one another in showing honour!" Romans 12:10. We have become so overwhelmed with the impression of his likeness in us, that any sense of lack, shortcoming or inferiority is challenged, even in the face of the most severe contradiction.

The object of New Testament ministry is not in the first place to get people to go to heaven one day! It is the unveiling of the most attractive life possible, the life of our design redeemed again. Now to be enjoyed in an immediate, intimate, daily, constant, conscious feedback encounter with the Living God in Spirit and in truth and undiluted friendship with our fellow humanity!

This is the bread that we daily feast on!

The prophetic picture of the table was most significant! The priests had to daily place fresh bread on the table in the sanctuary. It was called Showbread, lechem haPānīm, literally: "Bread of the Presence". The Hebrew word for presence means face to face! While Jesus spoke to the two men on their way to Emmaus in Luk 24, they did not recognize him, even though their hearts ignited while he was explaing the prophetic promise of mankind's redemption in all of scripture, from Moses through the Psalms and the prophets. In Luke's interview, he pressed them for the detail, he wanted to know exactly at what point in their meeting with Jesus did they recognise him in person! He writes in verse 28, "So they drew near to the village to which they were going. He appeared to be going further..." Wow! Should Jesus not at this point have given them an opportunity to make a comitment or at least say a "sinners prayer"? Not even the best Rabbi could take them any further, Luk 24:29 But they constrained him, saying, "Stay with us, for it is toward evening and the day is now far spent." So he went in to stay with them. Luk 24:30 When he was at table with them, he took the bread and blessed, and broke it, and gave it to them. Luk 24:31 And their eyes were opened and they recognized him; and he vanished out of their sight.

The moment we discover Jesus in scripture as in a mirror, our hearts ignite and our very next meal becomes a celebration of the incarnartion! "Every time you eat or drink, remember me!" Every meal celebrates the temple! Your body is God's address on planet earth! He does not dwell in buildings made by human hands. You will never again need to employ your willpower to diet and get into shape! Willpower is the language of the law! Love and value-consciousness ignites belief. The revelation of the truth sets you free to be free indeed! The days of fast food and junk-food are over! The Table is sacred and celebrates your body as the sanctuary of your redeemed life, the life of your authentic design! Eat food that blesses the temple! Most diseases are diet-related! Study nutrition! We have this treasure in earthen vessels! The vessel takes its value from the treasure it holds!

One day, having walked for at least twenty miles on a warm summer day, Jesus sent his disciples along into Sychar, a city of Samaria, to buy food. He waited for them besides the well of Jacob on the outskirts of the village. He felt exhausted, from the walk and thirsty.

A Samaritan woman eventually arrived at the well to draw water, and immediately he asked her for a drink. He had nothing to draw with and the well was about 150 feet deep. Recognizing Jesus as a Jew, she immediately began to exploit his predicament and reminded him that Jews were not supposed to speak to Samaritans. She was hoping to at least get some mileage out of the politics of her day.

The life Jesus lived in a human body was no different to ours; he felt the same weariness, hunger and thirst we would, yet he never forgot what manner of man he was. He lived convinced and conscious of who he was. This was his secret; this was how he overcame every temptation victoriously.

When she remarked about his Jewish identity, he said to her, "Woman if you knew the gift of God, and who he is who asked you for a drink, you would have asked him and he would give you water that becomes in you an artesian well."

In conversation with him this lady began to realize that Jesus was more than a Jew and that mirrored in him, she was more than a Samaritan. Suddenly she understood that all people indeed share the same origin. The fountain of living water was not distant from her, beyond her reach, but waiting to awaken within her. Not any of her previous five marriages or even her religious tradition could quench her thirst. Not because she failed to meet 'Mr. Perfect' or the men in her life failed to meet her expectation, but simply because of the fact that a partner was never meant to define or complete her life. Life is not defined by marriage, says Paul in 1 Cor 7. (See Mirror Bible)

The life of our design is defined in Jesus Christ as in a mirror. Here, there remains no partner, politics or past experience to blame or compete with, only a new life within you to discover, explore, enjoy and share. Your source will sustain you. "By the waters of reflection, my soul remembers who I am." Ps 23

Truth therapy does not attempt to untangle the complicated emotional hurts and traumas of the past; instead truth reveals the integrity of our original life redeemed in Christ. He is the fountainhead of our genesis. Paul did not say, "Behold the old! He said, "Behold all things are new!" 2 Cor 5:17

"Are you bigger than our father Jacob, who gave us this well?" In her encounter with Jesus her familiar religious identity is dramatically challenged. Everyone who drinks from the wells of religion will thirst again!

The business of religion desperately needs paying and returning customers! They crucified Jesus for this reason; their entire system of keeping people dependent on their hierarchy was challenged and condemned! So many sincere Christian ministries today fall into the same snare.

Jesus has no hidden agenda: "Whoever drinks from the water that I give shall never thirst again, because the water that I give becomes an artesian well within you!" Now this is economic ministry! This is what Paul knew when he wrote "Not only in my presence, but much more in my absence, discover the full extent of salvation in your own heart!" Phil 2:12. "Much more in my absence!" There is something more beneficial to the individual than Paul's next epistle or even his next visit! It is discovering the fountain within your innermost being! The unveiling of Christ in you completes your every expectation! Col 1:27.

The moment everyone was waiting for has come! From now on worship is no longer a geographic holy mountain- or holy city in Israel experience! It is not whether you are in Jerusalem or Johannesburg! The days of prophetic promise and delay are over! The hour has come and now is where neither on this mountain nor in Jerusalem will you worship the Father! You worshiped in ignorance; the true worshippers now worship the Father in spirit and in truth. The Father is our true fountainhead! Your true father is not your earthly father, neither Jonah nor Jacob! You are not defined by your physical birth, your history, culture or religion! "Blessed are you son of Jonah, for flesh and blood did not reveal this to you." I say you are Rock and upon this Rock I will establish my visible identity! The rock represents the revelation that the son of man is the son of God! Math 16:13, Hades will not prevail! Hades is a compound word from, ha, negative and ideis, to see. Man's ignorance of his true identity will not prevail!

The end of an era has arrived! Return to your Source. "He is the Author and conclusion of faith." Heb.12:2.

"Of God are you in Christ; He is the source of your life in Christ Jesus." 1 Cor 1:30 "Of God's doing are we in Christ. He is both the genesis and genius of our wisdom; a wisdom that reveals how righteous, sanctified and redeemed we already are in him." *(In God's economy, Christ represents us; what man could never achieve through personal discipline and willpower as taught in every religion, God's faith accomplished in Christ. Of his design are we in Christ; we are associated in oneness with him. Our wisdom is sourced in this union! Also our righteousness and holiness originate from him. Holiness equals wholeness and harmony of man's spirit, soul and body. Our redemption is sanctioned in him. He redeemed our identity, our sanity, our health, our joy, our peace, our innocence and our complete well-being!)* "All this is from God" 2 Cor 5:18. "We are his workmanship, created in Christ Jesus." Eph 2:10.

1 Cor 1:10 My dear Brothers, because we are surnamed and identified in the name of our master Jesus Christ, I [1]urge you to speak with one voice, (to say the same thing) we share the same source as our reference; no division or any sense of distance is tolerated, which makes us a perfect match, accurately joined in the same thought pattern and communicating the same resolve. *(The word, [1]parakaleo, is from para, a preposition indicating close proximity, a thing proceeding from a sphere of influence, with a suggestion of union of place of residence, to have sprung from its author and giver, originating from, denoting the point from which an action originates, intimate connection and kaleo, to surname.)*1 Cor 1:11 Some of the believers in Chleo's fellowship told me about the controversy in your ranks; this is most disturbing!

1 Cor 1:12 What I was told is that you are divided into groups, where some side with Paul, others with Apollos, still others with Kefas, and even some who say, "we are the Messianic group!"

1 Cor 1:13 This is really ridiculous: can Christ be cut up into little relics? Was Paul crucified for you? Were you baptized into Paul's name?

1 Cor 1:14 Baptism is not my business or emphasis; I am glad that I only baptized Crispus and Gaius amongst you! *(Crispus was his neighbor and leader of the synagogue [see Acts 18:8]. Gaius resided at Corinth. Paul stayed with him when he wrote the Epistle to the Romans [Rom 16:23]; he was also a travel companion of Paul's [Acts 19:29].)*

1 Cor 1:15 I distance myself from the idea of employing baptism as a means of branding my ministry with my name!

1 Cor 1:16 O yes! Now I remember that I also baptized the family of Stephanus. *(In 1 Corinthians 16:15, the family (young and old) of Stephanus were the first converts in Achaia)*

1 Cor 1:17 My mandate was not about winning members for some 'Christian club' through baptism! I am commissioned to declare the good news without any strings attached; nothing to distract from the powerful effect of the revelation of the cross of Christ. *(The mystery of the cross is the revelation of mankind's inclusion in his death and resurrection [see 1 Cor 2:7].)*

There is only one body, one faith and one fellowship, Eph 4:4-6. We do not invent fellowship, we are invited into the fellowship of the Father and the son! Our fellowship is founded in the communication that promotes and ignites the knowledge of every good thing that is in us in Christ. Philemon 1:6. Any communication that distracts from this reality is irrelevant.

When Paul first arrives in Ephesus he finds disciples of John the Baptist there, many years after their leader was murdered. They have never even heard of the baptism of the Holy Spirit, and were still preaching a doctrine of a sin-consciousness. Acts 19:1-6. While the disciples of Jesus were feasting and drinking, the disciples of John were fasting and praying. Luke 5:33. John the Baptist announced Jesus to be the Lamb of God, who takes away the sins of the world, he saw the heavens open above him and witnessed the Holy Spirit upon him in the form of a dove and heard the voice of God. Yet instead of becoming the first disciple of Jesus, he continued his own ministry. He continued to preach sin and condemnation as if the Lamb did not really take away the sin of the whole world. The title of his message says it all: "You brood of vipers…!"

The very portion of scripture he proclaimed under the prophetic unction of the Spirit, from Isaiah 40:3, begins with the words, in verse 1 and 2: "Comfort, comfort my people, says your God. Speak tenderly to Jerusalem and cry to her that her warfare is ended and her iniquity is pardoned!" Sadly, the ministry of guilt and condemnation seems to be blind to the good of the gospel. Condemning Herod's lust after his brother's wife landed John in prison. Doubt and offence begins to haunt him and from prison he sends his disciples to ask Jesus, "Are you the one who is to come, or shall we look for another?" Jesus answers them, "Go tell John what you see and hear: the blind receive their sight and the lame walk, lepers are cleansed and the deaf hear, and the dead are raised up, and the poor have good news preached to them. And blessed is he who takes no offence at me." Math 11:2-6. Whatever offends you neutralizes you.

John's reaction in prison is in sharp contrast to Paul's; neither were they in jail for the same reasons. John did not get jailed for his association with Jesus. While Jesus made friends with sinners, John condemned them. Paul went to jail often, and every time for the same reasons and by the same religious people who crucified Jesus. He tells his own story: "I have been imprisoned many times, and received countless beatings, often near death. Five times I was beaten 39 lashes. (In the movie, "The passion of Christ", Mel Gibson graphically portrays what happens to the human body when whipped thirty nine times!) Three times beaten with rods; once I was stoned; three times I have been shipwrecked; a night and a day adrift at sea; on frequent life threatening journeys, in danger from flooded rivers, danger from robbers, danger from my own Jewish people, danger from the Romans, danger in the city, danger in the wilderness, danger at sea, danger from false brethren; in toil and hardship, through many a sleepless night, in hunger and thirst, often without food, in cold and exposure." 2 Cor 11:23-28.

This testimony fills one with horror, yet Paul sees it this way: In all these things we are more than conquerors. He encounters a life flooded with joy in the face of severe contradiction!

2 Cor 4:17 We are fully engaged in an exceedingly superior reality; the extent and weight of this glory, which is God's redeemed image and likeness in us, makes any degree of suffering vanish into insignificance! The suffering is fleeting and ever so slight by comparison to the substance and enduring effect of this glory we participate in for all eternity. 2 Cor 4:18 We are not keeping any score of what seems so obvious to the senses in the natural realm, it is fleeting and irrelevant; it is the unseen eternal realm that has our full attention and captivates our gaze!

We are given a glimpse of the depth of Paul's insight into the mystery, of Christ revealed in him: "Rejoice always, and again I say, rejoice! I do not complain of lack, for I have learned, in whatever state I am, to remain unsettled in my conviction of my completeness in Christ. When people gossip about me or praise me; in any and all circumstances I have learned the secret of facing a feast and hunger; of having abundance and of being in lack: I can do all things through Christ who energizes me!" Phil.4:11-13.

Abundance is not proof of God's goodness; neither is lack the evidence of his absence! No extreme in any definition can challenge or diminish our completeness and union with our Father.

Competition is not what makes of you a champion; to realize how complete you already are by design and redemption in the face of contradiction, without any external confirmation or applause, is the true character of a champion.

It does not matter how imperfect, incomplete or in lack you might feel; the true gospel-mirror of the face of your birth reveals that by design and by the work of Jesus on the cross and in his resurrection, you are perfect and complete and lacking in nothing!

Jas 1:2 Temptations come in different shapes, sizes and intervals, their intention is always to suck you into their energy field. However my brothers, your joy leads you out triumphantly every time. *(The Greek word James uses here, hegeomai, is the strengthened form of ago, to lead; thus, to officially appoint in a position of authority, to lead with distinguished authority. "Count it all joy" make a calculation to which joy can be the only logical conclusion.)*

Jas 1:3 Here is the secret: joy is not something you have to fake, it is the fruit of what your faith knows to be true about you! You know that the proof of your faith results in persuasion that remains constant in contradiction.

Jas 1:4 *(Just like a mother hen patiently broods over her eggs,)* steadfastness provides you with a consistent environment, and so patience prevails and proves your perfection; how entirely whole you are and without any shortfall.

Jas 1:5 The only thing you could possibly lack is wisdom. *(One might sometimes feel challenged beyond the point of sanity)* however, make your request in such a way that you draw directly from the [2]source *(not filtered through other opinions).* God is the origin and author of wisdom; he [1]intertwines your thoughts with good judgment. His gifts are available to all, without regret. *(The word, [1]haplous, from ha, particle of union (hama, together with) + pleko, meaning to plait, braid, weave together. See Matthew 6:22, "If your eye is entwined with light your whole body will be full of light." Wisdom that comes from above remains unaffected by the contradictions of the senses. The word, [2]didomi, to give, to be the author or source of a thing — Wesley J. Perschbacher.)*

Jas 1:16 My dear brothers, do not go wandering off into deception. *(By giving credit to temptation, thinking that it could be God's way of speaking to you!)*

Jas 1:17 Without exception God's gifts are only good, its perfection cannot be improved upon. They come [1]from above, *(where we originate from)* proceeding like light rays from its source, the Father of lights. With whom there is no distortion or even a shadow of shifting to obstruct or intercept the light; no hint of a hidden agenda. *(The word, ¹anouthen, means, from above [Jn 3:3, 13]. Man is not the product of his mother's womb; man began in God.)*

Jas 1:18 It was his delightful ¹resolve to give birth to us; we were conceived by the ²unveiled logic of God. We lead the exhibition of his handiwork, like first fruits introducing the rest of the harvest he anticipates. *(The word, ¹boulomai, means the affectionate desire and deliberate resolve of God. Truth, ²alethea, from a, negative + lanthano, meaning hidden; that which is unveiled; the word of truth.)*

Jas 1:19 Consequently, my beloved brethren, *(when you are faced with temptation and contradiction)* ponder the Word that reveals your true origin, do not ponder the problem; that is how frustration is conceived. Rather remain silent than to give anger your voice. *(Quick to hear, slow to speak, slow to anger.)*

Jas 1:22 Give the word your ¹undivided attention; do not underestimate yourself. ³Make the calculation. There can only be one logical conclusion: your authentic origin is mirrored in the word. You are God's poem; ²let his voice make poetry of your life! *(The word, ¹akroate, means intent listening. James is not promoting the doing of the law of works; he is defining the law of perfect liberty. Doing the word begins with your undivided attention to the face of your birth. ²A doer of the Word, poetes, means poet. Make the calculation, ³paralogizomai, from para, a preposition indicating close proximity, union, and logizomai, to reckon the logic in any calculation.)*

Jas 1:23 The difference between a mere spectator and a participator is that both of them hear the same voice and perceive in its message the face of their own genesis reflected as in a mirror;

Jas 1:24 they realize that they are looking at themselves, but for the one it seems just too good to be true, he departs *(back to his old way of seeing himself)* and immediately forgets what manner of person he is; never giving another thought to the one he saw there in the mirror.

Jas 1:25 The other one is ¹mesmerized by what he sees; he is ²captivated by the effect of a law that frees man from the obligation to the old written code that restricted him to his own efforts and willpower. No distraction or contradiction can dim the impact of what he sees in that mirror concerning the law of perfect ³liberty *(the law of faith)* that now frees him to get on with the act of living the life *(of his original design.)* He finds a new ³spontaneous lifestyle; the poetry of practical living. *(The law of perfect liberty is the image and likeness of God revealed in Christ, now redeemed in man as in a mirror. Look deep enough into that law of faith that you may see there in its perfection a portrait that so resembles the original that he becomes distinctly visible in the spirit of your mind and in the face of every man you behold. I translated the word, ¹parakupto, with mesmerized from para, a preposition indicating close proximity, originating from, denoting the point from which an action originates, intimate connection, and kupto, to bend, stoop down to view at close scrutiny; ²parameno, to remain captivated under the influence of; meno, to continue to be present. The word often translated as freedom, ³eleutheria, means without obligation; spontaneous.)*

Jas 1:26 Meaningless conversation is often disguised in religious eloquence. Just because it sounds familiar or sincere, doesn't make it true. If your tongue is not bridled by what your heart knows to be true about you, you cheat yourself.

Eph 4:7 The gift of Christ gives dimension to grace and defines our individual value. *(Grace was given to each one of us according to the measure of the gift of Christ.)*

His grace reveals his redeemed likeness in us; this is the measure of our perfection and completeness. John 1:16 He is the source of our completeness. ¹Grace against grace! *(¹garin anti garitos, grace undeserved. Grace prevailed against the tide of darkness due to Adam's fall. His fullness is the source of all that grace communicates as our portion, against all odds!)*

Just like any student would first be qualified in passing their exams before they are to tackle the very real and demanding challenges of their career, it is important to become absolutely aquainted with the revelation of the mystery of Christ in you! In Paul's final letter to the Corinthians, he challenges the believers to examine themselves, to see whether they are holding to their faith. He says: "Test yourselves, do you not realize that Jesus Christ is in you?" 2 Cor 13:5 This realization is your starting point, not your goal! The test is not to determine whether Jesus Christ is present or absent in you; the test is to endorse the fact of his indwelling! With any exam there can always only be one correct answer; to examine yourself in the context of the good news, the law plays no roll! When Habbakuk announces our redeemed innocence by what God's faith sees, he challenges the sin-conscious based scrutiny of the Old Covenant.

Hab 3:17 Though the fig tree do not blossom, nor fruit be on the vines, the produce of the olive fail and the fields yield no food, the flock be cut off from the fold and there be no herd in the stalls,

Hab 3:18 yet I will rejoice in the LORD, I will joy in the God of my salvation.

Hab 3:19 GOD, the Lord, is my strength; he makes my feet like hinds' feet, he makes me tread upon my high places. To the choirmaster: with stringed instruments.

Any contradiction that can get you to forget your true identity, innocence and worth defeats you.

Religion over the years has majored on the subject of sin-consciousness. The moment something goes wrong, guilt trips are empowered. Simon's response surprises after he witnesses the teaching and ministry of Jesus, and a catch that he could not claim any credit for! "Depart from me Lord, for I am a sinful man!" He apparently felt a lot more familiar and comfortable to account the previous night's toil and no success to his own sinfulness! Karma makes so much sense to a religion that makes its money out of paying and returning customers!

Rom 1:17 Herein lies the secret of the power of the Gospel; there is no good news in it until the [1]righteousness of God is revealed! The dynamic of the gospel is the revelation of God's faith as the only valid basis for our belief. The prophets wrote in advance about the fact that God believes that righteousness unveils the life that he always had in mind for us. "Righteousness by his *(God's)* faith defines life." *(The good news is the fact that the Cross of Christ was a success. God rescued [1]the life of our design; he redeemed our [1]innocence. Man would never again be judged righteous or unrighteous by his own ability to obey moral laws! It is not about what man must or must not do but about what Jesus has done! It is from faith to faith, and not man's good or bad behavior or circumstances interpreted as a blessing or a curse [Hab 2:4]. Instead of reading the curse when disaster strikes, Habakkuk realizes that the Promise out-dates performance as the basis to man's acquittal. Deuteronomy 28 would no longer be the motivation or the measure of right or wrong behavior! "Though the fig trees do not blossom, nor fruit be on the vines, the produce of the olive fail and the fields yield no food, the flock be cut off from the fold and there be no herd in the stalls, yet I will rejoice in the Lord, I will joy in the God of my salvation. God, the Lord, is my strength; he makes my feet like hinds' feet, he makes me tread upon my high places [Hab 3:17-19 RSV]. "Look away [from the law of works] unto Jesus; he is the Author and finisher of faith." [Heb 12:1].*

The gospel is the revelation of the righteousness of God; it declares how God succeeded to put mankind right with him. It is about what God did right, not what Adam did wrong. The word righteousness comes from the Anglo Saxon word, "rightwiseness;" wise in that which is right. In Greek the root word for righteousness is [1]dike, which means two parties finding likeness in each other. The Hebrew word for righteousness is [1]tzadok, which refers to the beam in a scale of balances. In Colossians 2:9-10, It is in Christ that God finds an accurate and complete expression of himself, in a human body! He mirrors our completeness and is the ultimate authority of our true identity.)

Rom 8:29   He pre-designed and engineered us from the start to be jointly fashioned in the same mold and image of his son according to the exact blueprint of his thought. We see the original and intended pattern of our lives preserved in his Son. He is the firstborn from the same womb that reveals our genesis. He confirms that we are the invention of God. *(We were born anew when he was raised from the dead! [1 Peter 1:3] His resurrection co-reveals our common genesis as well as our redeemed innocence. [Rom 4:25 and Acts 17:31] No wonder then that he is not ashamed to call us his brethren! We share the same origin [Heb 2:11], and, "In him we live and move and have our being, we are indeed his offspring!" [Acts 17:28].)*

Rom 8:30 Jesus reveals that man [1]pre-existed in God; he defines us. He justified us and also glorified us. He redeemed our innocence and restored the glory we lost in Adam. *(As in Romans 3:23, 24; [1]prooritso, pre-defined, like when an architect draws up a detailed plan; kaleo, to surname, identify by name.)*

Rom 8:31 All these things point to one conclusion, God is for us! Who can prevail against us?

Rom 8:33 God has identified us, who can disqualify us? No-one can point a finger; He justified us. Rom 8:34 What further ground can there possibly be to condemn man? Christ died, this cannot be undone! His resurrection cannot be wished away. He occupies the highest seat of authority at the right hand of God in our favour. Rom 8:35 What will it take to distance us from the love of Christ? You name any potential calamity: intense pressure of the worst possible kind, cluster-phobia, persecution, destitution, loneliness, extreme exposure, life-threatening danger, or war? Rom 8:37 On the contrary, in the thick of these things our triumph remains beyond dispute. His love has placed us above the reach of any onslaught.

Rom 8:38 This is my conviction, no threat whether it be in death or life, be it angelic beings, demon powers or political principalities, nothing known to us at this time, or even in the unknown future; Rom 8:39 no dimension of any calculation in time or space, nor any device yet to be invented, has what it takes to separate us from the love of God demonstrated in Christ. Jesus is our ultimate authority.

Jas 1:2 Count it all joy, my brethren, when you meet various trials,

Jas 1:3 for you know that the testing of your faith produces steadfastness.

Jas 1:4 And let steadfastness have its full effect, that you may be perfect and complete, lacking in nothing. RSV

Steadfastness is the fruit of what your faith knows to be true about you. You cannot buy steadfastness over the counter, nor have someone lay hands on you to give you steadfastness; it comes no other way. To be convinced about your true identity and oneness with God, is the secret to the most sought-after quality of life beyond lack. A test or temptation in this context means anything that makes you feel imperfect, incomplete and in lack; anything that would challenge your conviction that Christ is in you. Remember, God tests no one; there is no hidden agenda with God, no shadow of inconsistency or change of mind. God is convinced about you. His mind is made up about you. His opinion of you is not subject to your passing or failing a test. He is in no need to still experiment with you because he already fully approves of you.

For you to be double minded is to be cheated out of steadfastness and to deceive yourself; you cannot afford that, not for any reason, no matter how many valid excuses you may have. "Let steadfastness have its full effect so that you may be perfect and complete, lacking in nothing." The Greek word James uses here for complete, holokleroi, means to be in complete possession of your allotted portion. Compare James 1:15, hamartia from ha-meros: to fail to possess your allotment, the full measure of life God intended for you, traditionally translated: sin. What is commonly proclaimed as sinful is often the mere symptom of an unfulfilled life. "To the hungry, everything that is bitter, seems sweet; but he who is satisfied, loathes honey." Proverbs 27:7. "The boundary lines have fallen for me in pleasant places, I am well content with my inheritance." Psalm 16:6.

God desires to show more convincingly to the heirs of the promise, the unchangeable character of his purpose! Hebrews 6:17. He wants to bring an end to all dispute! There can be no intamcy or romance in an environment of suspicion, blame and regret!

"Count it all joy," is the Greek word, hegeomai which is the strengthened form of the word, ago, to lead as a shepherd leads his sheep. A shepherd in Bible days was a figure of authority. He had to defend his flock against the elements, robbers and wild animals. Thus, hegeomai means to be officially appointed, to be in command with official authority, to have the rule over. "Let joy take official charge over your circumstances." Joy is not a weak attempt of a smile, while you are actually licking your wounds and feeling sorry for yourself.

Joy is the dominant force of your spirit in the face of contradiction. The most sober calculation one can make is a conclusion, which always results in joy. Remember that joy is not something you do; it is the fruit of something you know. Joy understands that the life of your design is redeemed.

Joy is the voice of faith. Joy is the fruit to what faith knows to be true about you. When joy has the official authority, then anxiety, sighing, feeling sorry for one self, complaining, seeking sympathy, talking about your problems and comparing problems etc. are all out-ruled. These re-actions will trap you into weakness and inferiority.

One of the biggest problems in South Africa since the demoralising and destructive philosophy of Apartheid is the constant reference to the "Previously Disadvantaged." Although it is well meant, we will never succeed to empower people by emphasising and encouraging feelings of pity and blame. Nothing is more self-destructive than feeling sorry for oneself and blaming someone else. This is just another cruel attack on human dignity. It becomes so easy to point a finger to the past and to whatever and whoever is to be blamed. The sad reality is that the more we feel justified in doing that, the longer we remain neutralized, para-lyzed and impoverished through reproach.

Life is not about things we do not have, but it is all about discovering what we have restored to us through the success of the cross and the wealth of the revelation of Christ in us; we are complete in him. We lack nothing. Of his fullness have we all received! (Col 2:10) He defines our lives not Adam! Jesus died the last Adam's death; in him every Boer, Zulu and Xhosa died together; the old things have passed away! Behold the new has come. He is the fulfilment of God's dream for you; nothing you could ever wish to become or own can match who you already are and what you already have in him. 1 Cor 4:8, "Already you are filled! Already you have become rich! Without us you have become kings!" Paul says that we have become all of this not through his teaching but through the success of the cross of Christ. Paul is not our reference; Christ is! Thank God though for what Paul saw and wrote to awaken our un-derstanding! Eph 3:4, "When you read this you can perceive my insight into the mystery of Christ." 1 Co 4:8 You are already saturated, literally jam-packed to capacity; you cannot get any wealthier than what you are! You are royalty *(because of what happened to you in Christ,)* not because of Apollos or Paul! Oh that you might know this so that we may co-reign together with you! *(We are not ranked any differently because we taught you the good news! So do not try and make heroes of us while you reduce yourselves to mere supporters and spectators. See also 1 Cor 1:30 and 2 Cor 10:12. Paul is re-enforcing the message of how complete we already are in Christ as our only reference and point of departure.)* Mirror Bible

Joy is the voice of faith; joy sings instead of sighs. The effect of our con-versation is compared to the rudder of a ship, a massive vessel can be steered effortlessly; never underestimate the dynamics of conversation. James 3:2-4. It is a common habit to descend from a higher place *(of faith)*

to a lower *(of the senses)*, especially in conversation. *(Greek, peripipto, from, peri, surrounded + pipto, from petomai, to fly; thus, to descend from a higher place to a lower, to stop flying)*. However, if you want to be in perfect charge of your whole person, the best place to begin is to take charge of your tongue. *(To reflect the word that confirms your true genesis, James 1:18,19.)*

Jas 3:3 With bit and bridle we are able to direct the strong body of a horse; you see it's the little bit in the mouth that makes the difference! Jas 3:4 Consider the effect of a small rudder on a large ship, when the seasoned Captain skilfully steers that vessel on a straight course contrary to fierce winds and weather.

Even our thoughts are silent words that impact our health and total life attitude.

Anonymous

"Love gives truth its voice." Eph 4:15

"It is not possible to study Christ in any other context. He is the incarnation, hear him resonate in you! The truth about you has its ultimate reference in Jesus. *("The truth as it is in Christ." He did not come to introduce a new compromised set of rules; he is not an example for us but of us!)* Eph 4:21

Acknowledging every good thing that is in us in Christ, ignites the the fellowship of our faith. Philemon 1:6

"Let the word of Christ inhabit you in rich abundance." Col 3:16

Col.3:1 "Pursue with diligence the consequence of your co-inclusion in Christ. Relocate yourself mentally! Engage your thoughts with throne room realities; his resurrection co-raised you to the same position of authority, seated in the strength of God's right hand.

Col 3:2 Becoming affectionately acquainted with these thoughts will keep you from being distracted again by the earthly (soul-ruled) realm.

Col 3:3 Your union with him in his death broke the association with that world; the secret of your life now is the fact that your life is wrapped up with Christ in God.

Col 3:10 We stand fully identified in the new creation renewed in knowledge according to the pattern of the exact image of our Creator.

Col 3:11 The revelation of Christ in everyone gives identity to the individual beyond anything he could ever be as a Greek or a Jew, circumcised or uncircumcised, foreigner, savage, slave or free.

Col 3:16 Christ is the language of God's logic. Let his message sink into you with unlimited vocabulary, taking wisdom to its most complete conclusion. This makes your fellowship an environment of instruction in an atmosphere of music. Every lesson is a reminder, echoing in every song you sing, whether it be a Psalm (raving about God in praise and worship accompanied by musical instruments) or a hymn (a testimony song) or a song in the spirit (a new spontaneous prophetic song). Grace fuels your heart with inspired music to the Lord.

This word-wealth becomes the theme of your conversation; it is the inspiration of every instruction, every Psalm, and song of praise, or even new spontaneous songs in the spirit.

Many sincere people think that there is virtue in discussing problems and debating the detail of darkness under the disguise of being truthful and open. The truth that frees one to be free indeed is mirrored in Christ. The issue is not what Adam or we did wrong but what God did right! This is the life changing ingredient of the gospel. Rom.1:17. This is the word of truth that the Spirit of truth speaks. John 16:13.

In his death the old things have passed away, now, behold all things are new. 2 Cor 5:17. You cannot look east and west at the same time!

Forget the old; acquaint yourself with the new!

Your mind, as a mental faculty, entertains thought from two sources, the senses (including memories), or the spirit. Spirit knowledge comes from within, while your senses only relate to your external environment. Our thoughts inspire our feelings. Perception dictates.

Spirit knowledge is realized through resonance and faith. Faith is to your spirit what your senses are to your body. Faith perceives reality beyond the horizon of the senses. The Greek word, to understand, sunieimi, from sun, together with, and eimi, I am, suggests a joint-knowledge; a flowing together as of two streams. The word for conscience, suneidesis from sun + eido, to see the same. joint knowledge or reflection, to see together, which is the opposite to hades. Hades is a compound word from ha, negative and ideis, from eido, to see, thus, not to see. Thus conscience speaks of a joint seeing.

Prov 4:23 Keep your heart with all vigilance; for from it flow the springs of life. We are designed to live from our innermost being. Every authentic expression of life is sourced there! Jesus says in Jhn 7:37, that if we believe that he is what the scriptures are all about, then we will discover that we are what he is all about and rivers of living water will gush out of our innermost being! It is from the heart to the head! Out of your innermost being rivers awaken! Our faculties of hearing and seeing beyond the horizon of the senses are ignited thru the truth of the gospel. The essence of the good news that brings great joy to all of mankind is that God has succeeded in his love initiative to cancel every definition of distance and seperation! This is so much more than mere information; it is a revelation of our redeemed innocence and oneness; to this we are now renewed in the spirit of our minds which is our deepest seat of consciousness. "Then you will know that I am in my Father and you in me and I in you!" Jhn 14:20.

Oneness is not an elusive mystic goal to strive towards for the rest of our lives! So many sincere people have over the centuries wasted many a day and even a lifetime striving to live "towards", when we have all along already been liberated in the finished work of Christ, to live "from" completeness! Eph 3:4 In [1]reading these words you will perceive my [2]insight into the mystery of Christ. (The word, [1]anaginosko, suggests an upward knowledge; to know again, to recognize, to read with recognition. Insight, [2]sunesis, from sun + eimi, together "I am", a flowing together like two rivers.)

Sometimes one might feel totally exasperated in the face of severe challenges and contradictions. Your crisis cannot exhaust God!

When Israel feels neglected by God, he responds to them in Isa 40:27, Why do you say, O Jacob, and speak, O Israel, "My way is hid from the LORD, and my right is disregarded by my God"? Isa 40:28 Have you not known? Have you not heard? The LORD is the everlasting God, the

Creator of the ends of the earth. He does not faint or grow weary, his understanding is unsearchable. Isa 40:29 He gives power to the faint, and to him who has no might he increases strength. Isa 40:30 Even youths shall faint and be weary, and young men shall fall exhausted; Isa 40:31 but they who wait for the LORD shall renew their strength, they shall mount up with wings like eagles, they shall run and not be weary, they shall walk and not faint.

Here we see man reaching the limit of his physical strength and ability. In his youth, his strength peaks; but even the champion athlete becomes weary and faints with exhaustion. Many can relate to the experience of reaching a point where one feels totally overcome and paralysed with weakness. But here is good news for those who feel that they have reached the end of the road: "They that "wait" upon the Lord shall renew their strength, they shall mount up with wings as eagles, they shall run and not be weary, and they shall walk and not faint." This certainly suggests a new dimension of experience; while your spirit soars, your body seems to cope with a new found energy facing the routine of day-to-day living or even having to deal with the increased pace of a real demanding day or crisis.

Here is the key: WAIT upon the Lord. Waiting has never been my favourite occupation. In fact I cannot think of anything more boring to do. Until I discovered the meaning of the Hebrew word translated "wait". The word "kawa" means to be intertwined or platted together like in the making of a rope or a musical string, thus multiplying its breaking-strength, or altering its pitch!

Your mind is engineered to be compatible with your Maker's thoughts about you. You have the mind of Christ! We are designed to feast on God's thoughts! Nothing thrills more than having your thoughts entwined with God's thoughts about you. The kawa- or mirror-principle is really key to entering into God's rest; this is what the Sabbath is all about. The Sabbath is the seat of our redeemed identity, value, innocence and authority; it is the secret of our strength! This is where we cease from our own labor and efforts to justify ourselves. Our most brilliant or clumsiest attempt to prove, promote or disqualify ourselves are surpassed by his single act of righteousness! 1 Cor 2:6 The words we speak resonate revelation wisdom in those who understand how perfectly redeemed they are in Christ, this wisdom supersedes every secular kind; suddenly what once seemed wise and good advice has become useless information. *(All popular programs towards improved moral behavior are now outdated. "Of God's doing are we in Christ. He is both the genesis and genius of our wisdom; a wisdom that reveals how righteous, sanctified, and redeemed we already are in him." In God's economy, Christ represents us; what man could never achieve through personal discipline and willpower as taught in every religion, God's faith accomplished in Christ [1 Cor 1:30].)* 1 Cor 2:7 We voice words of wisdom that was hidden in silence for timeless ages; a mystery unfolding God's Masterful plan whereby he would redeem his glory in man. 1 Cor 2:8 Neither the politicians nor the theologians of the day had a clue about this mystery *(of mankind's association in Christ);* if they did, they would never have crucified the Lord whose death redeemed our glory!

History recorded the death of one man, eternity recorded the death of the human race. One has died for all; therefore all have died! 2 Cor 5:14. When he was made alive, we were made alive together with him and co-raised with him. He also led us (humanity) as trophies in his triumphant procession on high! We are seated together with him in heavenly places! Eph 4:8 and 2:5.

The incarnation reveals that nowhere in the universe is mankind more comprehensively represented than what we are in Christ Jesus in the immediate presence of God! This all happened while we were still indifferent and even hostile towards our Maker. Truth does not become true by popular vote! Our belief does not make something true; mankind's redemption was true before anyone but God believed it. Jesus is the author and perfecter of faith! To see what God sees and to know what he knows to be true about you, ignites faith. Paul says that it is from faith to faith! Rom 1:17. God's belief in you rubs off on you! There is only one faith that matters, not what we believe about God but what he believes about us! This is what the mirror message is all about: "By the waters of reflection, my soul remembers who I am!" Ps 23. The message incarnate is awakened again while we behold his glory mirrored within us, with unveiled faces! We remember because we have simply forgotten what manner of persons we are by design. God wrote the script of our DNA when he knitted us together in our mother's womb. His eternal knowledge of us is what inspired our individual design.

Isa 40:30 and 31 basically reflect the two laws that Paul refers to in Rom 3:27, the law of works and the law of faith. The law of works is governed by willpower; the law of faith is inspired by love. While the one exhausts, the other ignites. Love awakens belief. Gal 5:6 It is the secret of effective ministry; tapping into the well within you causes you to soar in a different dimension in the midst of routine life; it is adventure unlimited!

James encourages us to not merely glance at the mirror, but to fully engage and deeply ponder the face of our birth unveiled in his. James 1:22 Give the word your [1]undivided attention; do not underestimate yourself. [3]Make the calculation. There can only be one logical conclusion: your authentic origin is mirrored in the word. You are God's poem; [2]let his voice make poetry of your life! *(The word, [1]akroate, means intent listening. James is not promoting the doing of the law of works; he is defining the law of perfect liberty. Doing the word begins with your undivided attention to the face of your birth. [2]A doer of the Word, poetes, means poet. Make the calculation, [3]paralogizomai, from para, a preposition indicating close proximity, union, and logizomai, to reckon the logic in any calculation.)* Jam 1:23 The difference between a mere spectator and a participator is that both of them hear the same voice and perceive in its message the face of their own genesis reflected as in a mirror; Jam 1:24 they realize that they are looking at themselves, but for the one it seems just too good to be true, he departs *(back to his old way of seeing himself)* and immediately forgets what manner of person he is; never giving another thought to the one he saw there in the mirror. Jam 1:25 The other one is [1]mesmerized by what he sees; he is [2]captivated by the effect of a law that frees man from the obligation to the old written code that restricted him to his own efforts and willpower. No distraction or contradiction can dim the impact of what he sees in that mirror concerning the law of perfect [3]liberty *(the law of faith)* that now frees him to get on with the act of living the life *(of his original design.)* He finds a new [3]spontaneous lifestyle; the poetry of practical living. *(The law of perfect liberty is the image and likeness of God revealed in Christ, now redeemed in man as in a mirror. Look deep enough into that law of faith that you may see there in its perfection a portrait that so resembles the original that he becomes distinctly visible in the spirit of your mind and in the face of every man you behold. I translated the word, [1]parakupto, with mesmerized from para, a preposition indicating close proximity, originating from, denoting the point from which an action originates, intimate connection, and kupto, to bend, stoop down to view at close scrutiny; [2]parameno, to remain captivated under the influence of; meno, to continue to be present. The word often translated as freedom, [3]eleutheria, means without obligation; spontaneous.)*

James 1:5 The only thing you could possibly lack is wisdom. *(One might sometimes feel challenged beyond the point of sanity)* however, make your request in such a way that you draw directly from the [2]source *(not filtered through other opinions)*. God is the origin and author of wisdom; he [1]intertwines your thoughts with good judgment. His gifts are available to all, without regret. *(The word, [1]haplous, from ha, particle of union (hama, together with) + pleko, meaning to plait, braid, weave together. See Matthew 6:22, "If your eye is entwined with light your whole body will be full of light." Wisdom that comes from above remains unaffected by the contradictions of the senses. The word, [2]didomi, to give, to be the author or source of a thing — Wesley J. Perschbacher.)*

"With him is the fountain (origin) of life, in his light do we see the light" Psalm 36:9.Nothing will benefit your body more.

Anxiety cannot be justified where peace rules!

Discover the integrity of your authentic, individual value. This will enrich your life beyond your highest ambition. What we already are as revealed and mirrored in Christ far exceeds anything we could ever wish to become!

In this context Jesus says not to be anxious about what you shall eat and what you shall drink or even to worry about your clothes. Mathew 6:25-34. "Take no thought about what you shall eat," Jesus says! These thoughts consume most people. Every thought you 'take' brings with it its own energy and influence. Instead, engage your thoughts with throne room realities! You belong there; he seated you together with him in innocence and authority! Col 3:1-4

"Look at the birds: they neither sow nor reap nor gather into barns, and yet your heavenly Father feeds them. Are you not of more value than they? And who of you by being anxious can add a measure to your span of life? Why are you anxious about clothing?" This does not mean that there is any merit in poverty. Wearing shabby clothes is not a mark of spirituality: "Consider the flowers of the field, how they grow; they neither toil nor spin yet I tell you that not even Solomon, with all his wealth, could clothe himself in greater splendour."

There is certainly nothing wrong with sowing and reaping and gathering; it is a principle of life. But it is foolish to get yourself entangled in greed and anxiety in the process. In the context of our completeness in Christ our point of departure can never again be lack. The law of liberty sows with joy and reaps with gladness. Faith even sows in famine. Genesis 26:1+12.

To be love driven or law driven is the difference between sonship and slavery.

You cannot cleave to God and money at the same time; the one occupies the space of the other. Your heavenly Father knows that you need all these things. Occupy your mind with the awareness of your oneness rather than with anxiety about things. The love of money makes people 'funny'. It is the weakest measure of value. Your worth is so much more than your job-description or salary. In your pursuit for fulfilment, "why do you spend your money for that which is not bread; and your labour for that which does not satisfy? Listen with undivided attention to me, and feast with delight on the fatness my words. O, every one who thirsts, come to the waters; and he who has no money, come buy and eat! Come, buy wine and milk without money and without price." Isaiah 55:1-3.

To walk in the light as he is in the light means to see your life and everything that concerns you, exclusively from your Father's point of view. You are indeed the focus of your Father's attention and affection. To be convinced of your origin in God is the vital energy of the law of liberty. To reflect the opinion of God in your attitude and conversation makes your life irresistibly attractive.

In the old days, training to become a teller in a bank, involved the habitual handling of real notes in order to become so acquainted with the feel of the real thing that a false note would immediately be detected. To teach your children what two plus two is not, is ridiculous. Teach them the truth, and they will naturally know the difference. For years we have been bombarded with sin, condemnation and guilt and have been told how unworthy and inferior we are; the inevitable result is more sin, condemnation, guilt and inferiority. Evil is neither immortal nor eternal, light is. Light remains the ultimate authority over darkness. There is no substitute for light. To discover yourself in the light of God's opinion is what truly sets you free.

To "die daily" makes no sense at all, if you are already decently dead. In the mind of God you died when Jesus died, once and for all. The "you" defined by your effort under the law of performance to justify yourself died. To come to the same conclusion and reckon your unenlightened-self to have died in his death is to agree with God. It is as simple as that. Romans 6:5,6,10,11. Your cross is not your partner, or your kids, or your boss; his cross is your cross. You are co-crucified with Christ. He died your death.

Paul's almost unbearable sufferings did not add any redemption value to the sufferings of Christ; nothing we suffer can contribute any merit to the validity and vital implication of the suffering of Christ on humanity's behalf. To punish your own body, by plucking out your eyes, cutting off your hands etc. could never add to the implications of the horror death Jesus suffered on your behalf. Col 1:24 "This is why no form of suffering can interfere with my joy. Every suffering on your behalf is just another opportunity to reinforce that which might still be lacking (in your understanding) of the affliction of Christ on behalf of his body which is the church." *(The inconvenience that Paul might be suffering on behalf of the believers is not to add to the sufferings of Christ - as though the sufferings of Christ on our behalf was insufficient but it is to further emphasize and confirm the principle of unselfish love that constrains N.T. ministry.)* Mirror Bible

The symptoms of flu, depression or any other illness or disease for that matter are always consistent. Rich or poor, famous or not, the symptoms appear the same in anyone. Whatever the symptom, it can never replace your person, at no point does it become you; it remains an intruder. The body is designed with an intelligent immune system to fight and resist any foreign intrusion. To judge or condemn your body when it feels ill or tired would be ridiculous. Learn to love yourself in the light of God's evaluation of you.

It is impossible to love yourself and die to yourself at the same time. There is absolutely no merit whatsoever in any attempt to die to yourself outside of realizing that you died the same death Jesus died. His resurrection reveals your new birth. 1 Peter 1:3. "After two days he will revive us, on the third day he will raise us up that we may live before him!" Hosea 6:2. (800 BC) "You are fearfully (awesome) and wonderfully made." Ps 139:14. "You are his workmanship." Ephesians 2:10 "His work is perfect." Deuteronomy 32:4.

If someone pays your debt simply because that person sees enough value in you to feel justified in doing that, then for you not to gratefully accept the gift would be an insult. Believe that God is right about you. He believes in you. His is the only faith that matters!

To soar in spirit dimension and share his vision for your life is your destiny and portion now! Mirror and mutter his thoughts concerning you continually; this is what it means to intertwine with him. Engage your thoughts with throne room realities. Col 3:1-3

Paul defines the secret of that which makes our fellowship and faith dynamic in Philemon 1:6, "The fellowship of your faith is ignited in the acknowledging of evey good thing that is in us in Christ!" Many find a "fellowship" in debating their problems etc.

The days of window-shopping are over! While the Old Testament is very much a display window of the new; the New Testament is the mirror. Window-shopping mode neutralized multitudes for many years into wishful thinking. Studying scriptures and "claiming" promises can keep one busy but not blessed. What happened historically and spiritually when Jesus suffered, died and was raised from the dead includes the whole of mankind, whether they believe it or not. "God was in Christ reconciling the world to himself." 2 Cor 5:19. God did not gamble with the life of his Son. God's righteousness is not at risk. His love is based on real value, not pity. In the incarnation he found the treasure where it was hidden all along, in the earthen vessel. No wonder then that he sold all he had and bought the field! Math 13:44 , 2 Cor 4:7. The "field" now is all he has! God has no other interest in the universe but you!

Only he knew the mystery that was hidden for ages and generations! The treasure in the earthen vessel is Christ in you! He redeemed his image and likeness in human form. He saw the fruit of the travail of his soul, and it satisfied him. God's faith sees you free!

Your new birth is not the result of a sincere decision you make to follow Jesus, but an awakening of your spirit to the truth of what already took place two thousand years ago when God raised Jesus from the dead. His resurrection from the dead included you! Hos 6:2, 1 Peter 1:3, Eph 2:5.

To merely see Jesus die historically as an individual carries no further significance beyond religious sentiment. Jesus is not an example for man; he is the example of man! "Beholding him as in a mirror, transforms our minds into his likeness, from glory (opinion) to glory (opinion)" 2 Corinthians 3:18. His opinion is the mould of our authentic design. The mirror reflects the death and resurrection of the one beholding. The mirror reflects mankind in Christ. This is the key to understanding the Gospel. See yourself mirrored in his death and in his resurrection. Romans 6:6.

To believe in the mineral wealth deposited in the earth is no guarantee against poverty. To discover gold in your own garden is what makes all the difference and sets one free. Find yourself in the Bible! This makes Bible reading exciting and life changing. Whenever we read the Bible we so often have someone else in mind!

When the scroll was handed to Jesus, he found the place where it was written: "The Spirit of the Lord is upon me, for he has anointed me to preach good news to the poor." His next statement startled the local audience; they thought they knew him so well, "Today this scripture has been fulfilled in your hearing!" Luke 4:17-22. The entire Bible is about

Jesus, and all of Jesus is about you! Heb 10:7 "Then I said, I read in your book what you wrote about me; so here I am, I have come to fulfil your will." (Ps.40:7, Luke 24:44.)

The revelation of the mirror changes everything. He mirrors me. This is how God sees me! When Jesus died, any excuse I could have to live an inferior life, died, and when he was raised, mankind was raised together with him into newness of life. In the mind of God, everything that Jesus did and everything that he is, includes the human race. The good news is simply a receipt offered to mankind as proof of their acquittal. His body on the cross represented the document of humanity's guilt; his resurrected and ascended body in the Throne room represents the receipt of humanity's acquittal.

It is amazing how we seem to struggle to receive something we did not work for or maybe argue that we do not deserve, yet we would have no problem claiming the money should we win the LOTTO. We also have no problem accepting the victory of our team or sport hero as our own: 'We won', we proudly proclaim, even though we only watched the game as a spectator. Yet we continue to reason that it will eventually take our own physical death to finally free us from the embarrassment of our body, as if Jesus' death only has spiritual and sentimental significance.

As if the first coming of Christ was a bit of a failure, another popular trap of religious thought and sentiment is to now desperately await the rapture and his second coming to rescue us.

The object of New Testament ministry is not in the first place to get people to go to heaven one day! It is the unveiling of the most attractive life possible, the life of our design redeemed again. Now to be enjoyed in an immediate, intimate, daily, constant, conscious feedback encounter with the Living God in Spirit and in truth and undiluted friendship with our fellow man!

He desires to communicate and reveal his image and likeness in you. In this sense and context you are his second coming! We are his body. The grain of wheat that would feed mankind with the true bread from heaven has fallen into the earth and died. It did not abide alone but produced an immeasurable harvest! John 12:24. This harvest is already ripe and ready! When Jesus said this, it was in response to the announcement that the Greeks want to see him; he knew that while limited to an individual body it is impossible to be in Jerusalem and Athens at the same time! You are God's harvest; the fruit of his labour.

Immediately after the resurrection, Peter and John gave to a cripple beggar what they had as a result of Christ's triumph. Instead of pointing the

106

man to an invisible historic or futuristic Jesus, Peter said, "Look at us! What we have, we give unto you!"

Mankind's inclusion in Christ's life, death and resurrection, is the restoration of all things that the prophets saw: "They proclaimed these days. God having raised up his son, sent him to you first." Jesus is not dead and gone; he is alive and well in every believer who embraces him as their true identity. The miracle of Acts 3 was more than the healing of the cripple; it was the fact that the risen Christ is now revealed in the lives of ordinary, uneducated, men! Acts 3:7,13,18-21,24,26. Acts 4: 13.

While I am still aware of a law within me, forcing me to think, speak or do things that would harm others or myself, I have already forgotten the word of truth that reveals the mirror image of my true identity. But then, to turn again to the fountain of truth, and perceive with awe the integrity of the law of my perfect liberty, confirms within me the unspeakable joy of oneness with my Maker. God's gift to mankind in Christ is out of all proportion to the effect of Adam's transgression. Rom. 5:12-21, 1 Cor. 15:21,22. We are convinced that one died for all, therefore all have died. From now on we no longer consider anyone from a human point of view. 2 Cor.5: 14,16.To hear that every good and perfect gift comes from God, and that we are his love dream, conceived in his image, is to see the face of our genesis as in a mirror. James 1:18,23,24. The Royal Law can only make sense in this context: Sharing an equal origin frees me to love and value my neighbour, as I love and value myself.

To practise hospitality and to show no partiality is the logical conclusion. Discover royalty, dressed in rags! James 2:1-4,8. How can we bless the Lord and Father, and then with the same mouth insult a man who is made in the likeness of God. James 3:9. It does not matter how much man appears to deserve insult, judgment and condemnation, in God's mind and in the light of what Jesus achieved, he deserves acquittal more. This is the good news in a nutshell.

"When the perfect comes, the imperfect will pass away. When I was a child I spoke like a child, I thought like a child, I reasoned like a child; when I became a man, I gave up childish ways. Now we see an enigma in a mirror, but then (when I became a man) face to face. As a child I know in part, but as a man I know even as I have always been known." 1 Cor. 13:10-13. God never knew man in any other light! The essence of the gospel is to know ourselves even as we have always been known. "As for me I shall behold your face in righteousness; when I awake, I shall be satisfied with beholding your form." Psalm 17:15.

2 Cor 3:18 The days of window-shopping are over! In him every face is [1]un-

veiled. In [2]gazing with wonder at the [5]blueprint likeness of God displayed in human form, we suddenly realize that we are looking at ourselves! Every feature of his [3]image is [2]mirrored in us! This is the most radical [4]transformation engineered by the Spirit of the Lord; we are led [6]from an inferior [5]mindset to the revealed [5]endorsement of our authentic identity. Mankind is his [5]glory! *(The word, [1]anakekalumeno, is a perfect passive participle from anakalupto; ana, a preposition denoting upward, to return again, and kalupto, to uncover, unveil. The word, [2]katoptrizomenoi, is the present middle participle from katoptrizomai, meaning to gaze into a reflection, to mirror oneself. The word [4]metamorphumetha is a present passive indicative from metamorpho; meta, together with, and meros, form. [The word commonly translated for sin, hamartia, is the opposite of this as ha, means without, and meros, form.] The word, [3]eikon, translates as exact resemblance, image and likeness; eikon always assumes a prototype, that which it not merely resembles, but from that which it is drawn; [5]doxa, glory, translates as mind-set, opinion from dokeo, authentic thought. Changed 'from glory to glory', apo doxes eis doxan; eis, a point reached in conclusion; [6]apo, away from, meaning away from the glory that previously defined us, i.e. our own achievements or disappointments, to the glory of our original design that now defines us. [Paul writes in Romans 1:17 about the unveiling of God's righteousness and then says it is from faith to faith. Here he does not use the word apo, but the preposition, ek, which always denotes source or origin.] Two glories are mentioned in this chapter; the glory of the flesh, and the unfading glory of God's image and likeness redeemed in us. The fading glory represented in the dispensation of the law of Moses is immediately superseded by the unveiling of Christ in us! Some translations of this scripture reads, "we are being changed from glory to glory." This would suggest that change is gradual and will more than likely take a lifetime, which was the typical thinking that trapped Israel for forty years in the wilderness of unbelief! We cannot become more than what we already are in Christ. We do not grow more complete; we simply grow in the knowledge of our completeness! [See Col 3:10] We are not changed "from one degree of glory to another," or step by step. How long does it take the beautiful swan to awaken to the truth of its design? The ugly duckling was an illusion! Whatever it was that endorsed the 'ugly duckling' mindset, co-died together with Christ!)*

LIFT OFF!!!

A little girl who had lost her front teeth, asked her teacher to take a bite into her apple, just to help her get "thtarted."

Without getting stuck in the do's and the don'ts, or falling into the trap of just another religious recipe, I would confidently encourage the following attitude:

Prayer is a love affair.

You have God's undivided attention! He so longs for yours!

Eph 6:18 Prayer is an ongoing conversation; praying in the spirit includes every form of prayer; whether it be a prayer of request or a prayer of thanksgiving, or worship, or interceding for all to realize their saintly innocence. Oh, and remember, you do not have to do all the talking! Always be attentive to the voice of the Spirit. *(Prayer is so much more than a one-way conversation.)* Phil 4:6 Let no anxiety about anything distract you! Rather translate moments into prayerful worship, and soak your requests in gratitude before God! Eph 5:19 Speak psalms to one another; burst out in spontaneous celebration songs and spirit-inspired resonance. In your heart do not let the music stop; continue to touch the Lord with whispers of worship.

Col 3:1 Engage your thoughts with throne room realities where you are co-seated with Christ in the executive authority of God's right hand. Col 3:2 Becoming affectionately acquainted with throne room thoughts will keep you from being distracted again by the earthly *(soul-ruled)* realm. Col 3:16 Christ is the language of God's logic. Let his message sink into you with unlimited vocabulary, taking wisdom to its most complete conclusion. This makes your fellowship an environment of instruction in an atmosphere of music. Every lesson is a reminder, echoing in every song you sing, whether it be a psalm *(raving about God in praise and worship accompanied by musical instruments)* or a hymn *(a testimony song)* or a song in the spirit *(a new spontaneous prophetic song)*. Grace fuels your heart with inspired music to the Lord. Col 3:17 Your every conversation and the detail of your daily conduct reflect him; his name and lordship define your lives and inspire your deep gratitude to God the Father.

Worship beyond religious routine. It is amazing how small your requests become when you become absorbed with his Person and his presence. Worship is simply an awareness of your oneness!

Even in our requests,our starting point is not the need but our persuasion of his perfect provision! We are not striving to gain God's attention or approval! We already enjoy his full attention and complete approval to begin with! Neither are we trying to get a "breakthrough"! The gospel reveals God's initiative in breaking through into our darkness with his amazing light! We love because he first loved us! 1 Jhn 4:19. He was ready to be found before we sought him! He said, "Here I am, here I am!"

Isa 65:1. Jesus is God's eternal, "Here I am" to the world!

God desires to be so much more in you than a 'quick-fix', spare-wheel solution. Allow his Being and the revelation of his provision and your inclusion in Christ, to overwhelm you. It is not the degree or severity of our needs that inspire fervent and effective prayer, but the persuasion and steadfastness of our faith in his accomplished work. Isa 40:27 Why do you say, "My way is hid from the LORD, and my right is disregarded by my God"? Isa 40:28 Have you not known? Have you not heard? The LORD is the everlasting God, the Creator of the ends of the earth. He does not faint or grow weary, his understanding is unsearchable. Isa 40:29 He gives power to the faint, and to him who has no might he multiplies strength. Isa 40:30 Even youths shall faint and be weary, and young men shall fall exhausted; Isa 40:31 but they who entwine their thoughts with the LORD shall renew their strength, they shall mount up with wings like eagles, they shall run and not be weary, they shall walk and not faint. *(The Hebrew word, **kawa** means to entwine, to be platted together.)*

Isa 40 begins with a level highway in the wilderness, just like a runway that is perfectly prepared to make it possible for an aircraft to easily become airborne: "Every valley shall be lifted up, and every mountain and hill be made low; every crooked place shall be made straight; even the rough places shall be made smooth!" In the incarnation, the word became flesh; the promise became a person, and in him God cancelled every definition of distance and every excuse mankind could possibly have to feel neglected or seperated from their Maker. The chapter then concludes with the kawa-principle where a new dimension of divine encounter is introduced: mounting up with wings like an eagle!

This place of intimate encounter is not meant for a select few; it is the life of our design redeemed again because of the success of the cross! Isa 40:5 And the glory of the LORD shall be revealed, and all flesh shall see it together, for the mouth of the LORD has spoken." God's glory is his workmanship, his image and likeness revealed and redeemed in human form! Jesus is the image of the invisible God; and we behold him, not as in a display window, but as in a mirror! The fulness of God bodily indwells him, and we are complete in him! Col 2:9,10.

Col 1:13 He rescued us from the [1] I am of darkness-idea, and relocated us into the kingdom where the love of his son rules. *(Darkness is not a force, it is the absence of light. [See Eph 4:18] A darkened understanding veiled the truth of our original design from us; 2 Cor 4:4. What "empowered" darkness was the lie that we believed about ourselves! The word, [1]exousia, sometimes translated authority, is from **ek**, origin or source, and **eimi**, I am. Thus, I was confused about who I am until the day that I heard and understood the grace of God in truth, as in a mirror. See 2 Cor 3:18, John 1:12.)*

Col 1:14 In God's mind mankind is associated in Christ; in his blood sacrifice we were ransomed; our redemption was secured; our [1]sins were completely done away with. *(The Greek word for sin, [1]hamartia is a compound word, **ha**, without, and **martia** from **meros**, form. Sin distorts the life of our design. Jesus revealed and redeemed our true form.)*

Col 1:15 In him the image and likeness of God is made visible in human life in order that every one may recognize their true origin in him. He is the firstborn of every creature. *(What darkness veiled from us he unveiled. In him we clearly see the mirror reflection of our original life. The son of his love gives accurate evidence of his image in human form. God can never again be invisible!)*

Col 1:16 Everything that is begins in him whether in the heavenly realm or upon the earth, visible or invisible, every order of justice and every level of authority, be it kingdoms or governments, principalities or jurisdictions; all things were created by him and for him.Col 1:17 He is the initiator of all things therefore everything finds its relevance and its true pattern only in him.

Col 1:18 The ekklesia *(church)* is the visible expression *(body)* of which Jesus is the head. He is the principle rank of authority who leads the triumphant procession of our new birth out of the region of the dead. His pre-eminent rank is beyond threat. *(" ... leading the resurrection parade"* — *The Message)*

Col 1:19 The full measure of everything God has in mind for man indwells him. *("So spacious is he, so roomy, that everything of God finds its proper place in him without crowding."* — *The Message)*

Col 1:20 He initiated the reconciliation of all things to himself. Through the blood of the cross God restored the original harmony. His reign of peace now extends to every visible thing upon the earth as well as those invisible things which are in the [1]heavenly realm. *(The heavens, [1]ouranos, a place of elevation, from **oros**, a mountain, from **airo**, to lift, to raise, to elevate, "Not only that, but all the broken and dislocated pieces of the universe, people and things, animals and atoms, get properly fixed and fit together in vibrant harmonies, all because of his death."* — *The Message.)*

"Ah Lord God! You have made the heavens and the earth by your great power and by your outstretched arm. Nothing is too difficult for you. Great and mighty God, you are great in counsel and mighty in deed. "Behold I am the Lord, the God of all flesh; is anything too hard for me?" Jeremiah 32:17,27.

It is so natural to delight yourself in the Lord when you knowthat his delight is in you. "Delight yourself in the Lord, and he will give you the desires of your heart." Psalm 37:4. Do not be snared by the deceitfulness of riches. Nothing fulfills more intimacy with God. Salute your Genesis with great reverence and respect. He is such a Gentleman. He schools us in the womb of his patience. He enables and anoints us. "He surrounds you with favour as with a shield." Psalm 5:12. Begin to live your wealth. With what you have already seen, you can be a powerful blessing to someone else. Remember how one boy's breakfast fed a multitude! Live a value-conscious life. Live aware of the wealth within you. When someone is really rich, they beam with confidence, without presumption or arrogance. They can afford to be humble; there is no need for them to be noticed or complimented. Mathew 6:2-4. God is pleased with you because he believes so much in himself in you. Your life is his design; his address.

Your faith reveals the value you place upon God's faith in you. To be overwhelmed with the awareness of God's indwelling, ignites and awakens the human spirit with a desire to be useful. Suddenly your immediate, personal needs seem insignificant in comparison to God's ability in you to reach out to others. No wonder that James conclude that true religion is to visit the widows and the orphans. Can you imagine how their discovery of their completeness in Christ would minister to them and free them from their grief and loneliness. Js 1:2-4, 27 Communicate gratitude, appreciation, affection, admiration, encouragement and value. Become a messenger of good news, exclusively. Do not argue. What is the use of winning the argument, but losing the person? Now you can afford 'to give without hesitation, to lose without regret and acquire without meanness.' George Sand Our ability to see value in another must be kindled, even if those values have become crusted over with corruption, fear, disappointment and hatred. The human spirit, enlightened by the reflection of the Spirit of our Maker, continues to be the dominant force against corruption and all manner of darkness. Suspicion and prejudice are overpowered by forgiveness, integrity and friendship. These are forces of light and life that can never be underestimated.

The greatest personal gain is to love and give without a thought for personal gain, to live to give, without side motives or any hidden agenda. Can you imagine a society where this attitude rules?

I used to own two old Leyland buses. The one was 30 and the other 50 years old. What always amazed me was how reliable these old buses were. At the mere press of a button, the engines crank, puff and with a thunderous roar, start; they were designed to do just that. People are designed to respond to touch. May this teaching touch you like the gentle rain upon the tender shoots, and like showers upon the strong herbs. Deuteronomy 32:2.

I will whisper words that the wind will take beyond; and time will turn to thunder in the cloudburst of thought. Time is the partner of the womb.

When my youngest son, Stefan was four years old, he stood on tippy-toe in order to reach the keyboard of the piano and played the very same tune he just heard his eldest brother, Renaldo played. I was startled and asked him how he did that, "It's easy, Dad, I just press the buttons that sound like the song!"

By the way, this same James who writes about the mirror image was the younger brother of Jesus. They worked as carpenters with their father and led a normal life within the accepted social structure of their time, for many years. But when Jesus turned 30, his extraordinary life and ministry began. Initially James must have struggled with a bit of an identity crisis. Where would his brother get all this talent from, all of a sudden?

Multitudes were attracted to hear him preach and witness his miracles. Ordinary water is nominated best wine at a wedding. In the same way ordinary people have their lives transformed. Many chronic diseases are miraculously cured. The blind weep with joy when they suddenly begin to see. The deaf hear, the lame leap and dance. Lepers are declared clean and even the dead are raised.

His reputation spreads abroad. So much so that people travel from overseas to meet him. Tourism gets a boost. Travel in those days was far from convenient. It was life threatening! Yet the Greeks arrive in Jerusalem and demand to see Jesus. John 12:19-24. His disciples are excited; they must give them value for their money. Maybe they could persuade him to do a quick miracle or two, like walking on water, or should they begin to line up the sick. What an opportunity to market their Master internationally!

But Jesus responds to the request of the Greeks with this startling statement: "The hour has come for the son of man to be glorified." What was he talking about? Would he now seize power and be crowned King of the Jews! He could possibly become the greatest political leader of all time?

Yet this was not to be the great moment for a great individual; this is the greatest moment for mankind!

"Unless the single grain of wheat falls into the ground and dies, it remains alone. But if it dies it bears much fruit!"

The fruit of God's act of righteousness reveals that the glory that Adam lost on humanity's behalf is redeemed again!

Jesus discovered himself mirrored in scripture and knew without a doubt who he was. Heb 10:7 "Then I said, I read in your book what you wrote about me; so here I am, I have come to fulfill my destiny." *(Ps 40:7, Lk 4:17, Lk 24:27, 44.)* When he heard about the Greeks having come all the way to see him, he heard the prophetic voice of Haggai 2:7 echo within him; he knew that he was the desire of the nations. Jesus understood that the revelation of the invisible God in a human body was never meant to remain the exclusive revelation of God in a single unique individual whose significance would in time fade to become a mere historic hero of religious sentiment. Neither was his mandate to be the Messiah of a single unique nation. His life, death and resurrection would represent the entire human race. "The earth is the LORD's and the fullness thereof, the world and those who dwell therein." Psa 24:1. The ends of the earth shall remember and turn to the Lord. Ps 22:27.

The same brother James admits in the first chapter of his book that we have forgotten what manner of man we are; we have become distracted and deceived by contradictions.

The greatest need for mankind is to hear the familiar voice of their Shepherd and to embrace his closeness. Their Maker is not a foreign, distant God. His name is Emmanuel, God with us! He is not more Emmanuel to the Jew than what he is to the Greek. He is not far from each one of us, in him we live and move and have our being! He is closer to us than the air we breathe; closer to us than our next thought!

The hour has come for the son of man to be glorified. The time of captivity and darkness is over. The harvest of all that God purposed and accomplished in his sacrificial death is here! The unveiled purpose of God now shines into our hearts to bring the liberating knowledge of our oneness with him. The mirror of truth reveals and reflects the glory (original opinion) of God restored in the flesh.

Rom 3:22 Jesus is what God believes about mankind. In him the righteousness of God is on display in such a way [1]that all may be equally persuaded about what God believes about them, regardless of who they are; there is no distinction. *(The preposition, [1]eis, indicates a point reached in conclusion.)*

Rom 3:23 Everyone is in the same boat; their [1]distorted behavior is proof of a [2]lost [3]blueprint. *(The word sin, is the word [1]hamartia, from ha, negative and meros, form, thus to be without form or identity; [2]hustereo, to fall short, to be inferior, [3]doxa, glory, blueprint, from dokeo, opinion, intent.)*

Rom3:24 Jesus Christ is proof of God's grace gift; he redeemed the glory of God in human life; mankind condemned is now mankind justified because of the ransom paid by Christ Jesus! *(He proved that God did not make a mistake when he made man in his image amd likeness! Sadly the evangelical world proclaimed verse 23 completely out of context! There is no good news in verse 23, the gospel is in verse 24! All fell short because of Adam; the same 'all' are equally declared innocent because of Christ! The law reveals what happened to man in Adam; grace reveals what happened to the same man in Christ.)*

Rom 3:25 Jesus exhibits God's mercy. His blood propitiation persuades humankind that God has dealt with the historic record of their sin. What he did vindicates God's righteousness.

Rom 3:26 All along God [1]refused to let go of man. At this very moment God's act of [2]righteousness is [3]pointing mankind to the evidence of their innocence, with Jesus as the [4]source of their faith. *(God's tolerance, [1]anoche, to echo upwards; God continued to hear the echo of his likeness in us. See Rom 2:4. In both these verses [25+26] Paul uses the word, [3]endeixis, where we get the word indicate from. It is also part of the root for the word translated as righteousness, [2]dikaiosune. To point out, to show, to convince with proof. Then follows, [3]ek pisteos iesou, ek, source or origin and iesou is in the Genitive case, the owner of faith is Jesus! He is both the source and substance of faith! Heb 11:1, 12:2)*

Rom 3:27 The law of faith cancels the law of works; which means there is suddenly nothing left for man to boast in. No one is superior to another. *(Bragging only makes sense if there is someone to compete with or impress. "While we compete with one another and compare ourselves with one another we are without understanding. [2 Cor 10:12]. "Through the righteousness of God we have received a faith of equal standing." [See 2 Pet 1:1 RSV] The OS (operating system) of the law of works is willpower; the OS of the law of faith is love. Gal 5:6 Love sets faith in motion. The law presented man with choices; grace awakens belief! Willpower exhausts, love ignites! If choices could save us we would be our own Saviors! Willpower is the language of the law, love is the language of grace and it ignites faith that leads to romance; falling in love beats "making a decision to believe in love"! See Rom 7:19)* Rom 3:28 This leaves us with only one logical conclusion, mankind is justified by faith and not by their ability to keep the law.

Now we all with new understanding see ourselves in him as in a mirror; thus we are changed from an inferior mindset to the revealed opinion of our true Origin. 2 Corinthians 3:18

Arise and shine for your light has come; the glory of the Lord is risen upon you! Isa 60:1

To now gaze with unveiled faces is to see the glory of God mirrored in your own eyes! 2 Cor 3:18. In the incarnation God has cancelled every definition and illusion of distance or separation! "And the glory of the Lord shall be revealed, and all flesh shall see it together!" Isa 40:3-5.

CHURCH

The teachings, miracles and fame of Jesus became a subject of much debate. What would the meaning of all this be?

"Who does man say that I the son of man am?" Jesus asks his followers. Matthew 16:13. Everybody knew that Joseph and Mary were the parents of Jesus. Or would Jesus possibly be a reincarnation of Moses or maybe the prophet Elijah? Simon suddenly speaks up with conviction, "You are the Christ, the Son of the living God!"

The Greek word for Christ, *xristos*, reminds of the word *xeir*, hand. The handbreadth was the earliest form of measure or blueprint. We still measure a horse to be, for example 17 hands high. This is also the root meaning of the Hebrew word, Messiah, *meshach*, to smear with the hand, to measure. When someone was identified as king or priest, oil was smeared over their head to annoint them and announce their authotity. The word Christ or Messiah means the anointed one. Jesus, means Saviour; He was prophesied to rescue the human race, since the beginning of recorded history. He is the hand of God that would interrupt time and reveal the eternal blueprint and measure of their original design. "We see the original and intended shape of our lives there in him." (The Message translation. Romans 8:29.)

"Blessed are you Simon son of Jonah, for flesh and blood did not reveal this to you, but my Father." You did not begin in Jonah. Now that you understand who I am, allow me to introduce you to you! "Call no man your father, mankind only has one father, the Father from whom every family in heaven and earth is named! Man began in God! Math 23:9, Eph 3:15 "I knew you before I formed you in your mother's womb!" Jer 1:5. "I tell you that you are Rock, (Petros) and on this Rock (petra, the greater rock, thus, petros hewn from the petra, Is.51:1) I will build my church, and the gates of Hades shall not prevail against my ekklesia." The church is the voice announcing the image and likeness of God redeemed and revealed in the flesh; the word was made flesh! The revelation that the son of man is indeed the Son of God is the fundamental mandate of the church. The word translated, church, ekklesia, says so much more than what the traditional picture that comes to mind, suggests. Two Greek words make up the word ekklesia: ek, is a preposition which always denotes origin or source, and the word kaleo, means, to surname, to identify by name.

The ekklesia is the unveiling of our original identity, freeing us to know ourselves even as we have always been known. 1 Cor 13:12. In Jesus God introduces us to ourselves again! Since Adam's fall mankind's perception of themselves have been confined to the flesh, dominated by the law of works and performance.

The word hades, from ha, negative, and ideis, means not to see. To see life merely as one dimensional through the natural eyes, is to be trapped into a bonsai mindset and existence. The phrase "the gates of hades shall not prevail against the ekklesia," suggests that the call to come out of this walled city of life in the flesh, protected by the senses as it were, will cause all resistance to crumble. Hades represents anything that imprisons man in an inferior opinion of himself. There awaits the most exciting life imaginable outside the walls of this city. The walls that were meant to locate and protect the city became a prison.

God's strategy for his church is not a building, but a body! Fellowship is so much more than a formal meeting; it is an ongoing conversation; it is the communication of every good thing that is in us in our union with Christ. Philemon 1:6. Acknowledging every good thing that is in us in Christ ignites the koinonia of faith! This remarkable simple statement defines fellowship better than anything that I have ever heard!

All the church buildings today, of all denominations, filled to capacity, could not even accommodate 2% of the world's population. God sees much more than an organisation or a building; he sees your body, as a practical, mobile vehicle that contains and reveals the presence and nature of an invisible God.

God has found a face in you that portray him more accurately than the best theology! Your features, your touch, the cadence of your voice, the compassion in your gaze, the lines of your smile, the warmth of your person and presence unveils him!

God sees a value in the individual equal to what he saw in Jesus. The grain of wheat produces a harvest according to its kind. The harvest is not a diluted, inferior immitation of the original seed; it is the exact mirror image of the same seed! Jesus said, "the works that I do, you will do also, and greater works, because I go to the Father." Jesus could only be at one place at one time, for three years of ministry. Now He is multiplied in us beyond time and restriction. This is God's strategy. This is the harvest he anticipates. For this purpose he equips the church with all that it takes to present every man in the full stature of Christ. Ephesians 4:11-13. God's purpose is to equip you with the revelation of his fullness in you so that your life will touch the next life with equal impact. People relate to people. Paul understands this strategy: "and our hope is that as your faith increases, our field among you will be greatly enlarged, so that we may preach the Gospel also in lands beyond you." 2 Cor 10:15,16. The invisible God makes himself visible, tangible and audible in you! Wow! Your body and person is his vehicle. You are God's strategy! Imagine God thinking his thoughts in your mind. Imagine God speaking his word through your lips. Imagine God doing his work through your hands! Imagine the eternal One employing your time! "The Spirit of the Lord is upon me to preach good news to the poor, to heal the broken hearted, to set the captives free and to open the eyes of the blind." Luke 4:18-19. This message does not come to you as another alternative, interesting perspective or a new interpretation of traditional doctrine. Neither does it offer you the option to trade in your 'skedonk' for a Mercedes. We are talking space ships here! A new dimension of dynamic life in the here and now is awakening within you.

While we were on honeymoon at Blydepoort, Mpumalanga (Jan 1979) Lydia and I met an official from Nature Conservation who told us of a fascinating incident; she witnessed the dramatic release of a Black Eagle a few weeks prior to our visit. This eagle had been captive in the Pretoria zoo for ten years. She told us how thrilled they were with excitement and anticipation when the eagle finally arrived in its cage and the gate was opened. But only with difficulty did they eventually succeed to nudge the bird out of its cage. It was one thing to get the bird out of the cage, but how do you get the cage out of the bird? In the mind of this eagle, it was still captive in the Pretoria zoo! Every one was holding their breath, but this once mighty bird remained the pathetic prisoner of an inferior mindset. Nothing changed until much later when another eagle began to call in the area. The eyes of the zoo-eagle immediately lit up, and the next moment she took off in majestic flight to soar in unrestricted space. When you hear the familiar voice, you no longer require flying lessons. The prison doors are open. Hades cannot hold you back. The ends of the earth shall remember and turn to the Lord! Ps 22:27.

EKKLESIA.

"YOU ARE GODS; YOU ARE ALL SONS OF THE MOST HIGH"

Next to the fact that Genesis 1:26 declares that God created man in his image and likeness, these words rank amongst the most startling statements on record in all of scripture. What makes it even more amazing is the audience Jesus addresses: The religious leaders of his day are so offended by him that they are about to stone him for blasphemy. How dare he, a mere son of man make himself equal to God? Statements such as "I and the Father are one" just did not go down well with the Pharisees! John 10:30-39. They would rather have him classified insane and demon possessed, or better still, destroy and silence him for ever. To these unenlightened religious fanatics Jesus quotes the prophet Asaph's words: "I say you are gods; you are all sons of the Most High, but you know nothing and understand nothing, why would you die like mere men." Psalm 82:5-7.

In spite of man's darkened understanding, mankind is the godkind by design. Man is not a separate creation detached from God; he is the very image bearer of God, equal in likeness and spirit capacity. He is in fact a part of God himself.

The scripture in Hebrews 2:6-12 is equally dynamic in content. Here even the translators of the text seem to be reluctant to identify man with God, they feel more comfortable with the word 'angels'. The eighth Psalm of David is quoted: "what is man, that you are mindful of him? What would attract you to the son of man that you would visit him? You made him a little lower than God" says the original text in Psalm 8, but the writer of the Hebrews epistle or more likely the one who copied the text felt more comfortable with, "a little less than angels."

"You crowned him with glory and honour. All things are placed under his control." We share in the substance and being of God; we are only limited in our understanding and perception. Yet the fall into sin plunged humanity into a place where instead of man ruling over the animal world, animal-like behavior often dictates to man.

Only when redemption-realities dawn in our understanding, is the dominance of an inferior identity broken.

In his Book, THE GOD-MEN, Dr John G Lake writes the following:

We have our physical body with its five sensory organs, and through these we are brought into contact with a certain range of activity that is purely physical. But that is not all there is to man. God desires an awakening of our understanding to realize that the man within is the real man. The spirit-man is the eternal undying man. It is the man whom God himself cannot destroy, because God cannot destroy himself. Man is of the very substance of God.

When man subjects that great God-man of the heart to the degradations of the desires of the outer fleshly man, how that inner man must groan. God never intended that the outer man of the flesh should be the governor of the great man of the spirit. Just as the outer man receives by impression, through contact, the things that occur about him, and as these are recorded in the soul, so the greater range of action of the spirit, through the spiritual senses, permits man to touch God Himself. He is able to touch the best things in the universe and bring them back in consciousness to the soul. The spirit man has a larger range of action than the physical man. Both the physical and the spiritual man record their facts in the soul consciousness.

The development of the inner man into the likeness and stature of Christ is the greatest element and purpose that can occupy our lives. The new force that takes hold of our heart is the consciousness that God has an eternal purpose in our life. A divine mission and purpose that will continue to unfold even beyond our life in the flesh.

I am a believer in the partnership of man and God. There is a fusing, a symphonising of God and man; the two become one. Not a saved man and a glorious God. But man fused into God and God fused into man, one divine creation. When Moses stood at the Red Sea, it was not Moses and God; it was just God. We say: "Lord make me a channel", leaving ourselves separated from God in our thought and expecting God to pour his spiritual power and blessing through us. That is not the highest thing. There is a greater experience than that in God's word: It is where you discover that you and God are one. Your whole body, your whole soul, your whole mind, your whole heart, your whole spirit begins to move in the rhythm and fusion and symphony of the eternal God; one in heart, one in mind, you and God as one. Moses tried to back out of this relationship. God told him to shut up and stop praying and to get on with the job! "...You stretch out your hand over the sea and you divide it!"

God is not merely looking for a place of residence; he is looking for a right of action in the body and spirit of man. God expects that same love union that is brought to pass between your soul and his own to be extended so that you embrace in that union every other soul around you. In your home, in your office, wherever you are, you leave the impress of your thoughts there. Wherever you are you manifest his sweetness and evidence his power.

The ultimate note of the gospel of Jesus Christ is to awaken every man, bound by sin and held by sensuousness and enslaved by the flesh, to discover themselves as sons of God. Not sons of God in a lower order, but sons of God as Jesus is. The human being is the most marvellous and wonderful instrument in all of creation in its capacity to reveal God.

People have so been in the habit of putting Jesus in a class by himself that they have failed to recognize that he has made provision for the same living Spirit of God that dwelt in his own life, and of which he himself was a living manifestation, to inhabit your being and mind. You are just as necessary to God in his plan for the salvation of mankind as God is necessary to you. Without man God would have no medium through which he could express himself to the world.

We have treated the precious Spirit of God as though he is a method of providing a means of spiritual entertainment. God's purpose is far mightier than that. When Jesus was about to depart, he said, "the glory that the Father gave me I give unto you. The works that I have done, you will do also and greater works." Unless Jesus was the possessor of a divine secret, a secret that others did not understand, such words as these would be words of madness. But because Jesus understood the secret of the Father's promise and purpose, he was able to make these marvellous statements.

John G. Lake was an American preacher, greatly used of God in South Africa and also in the United States in the early 1900's.

What men of his generation had to say about John Graham Lake:

"Dr Lake's teaching will eventually be accepted by the entire world."

Mahatma Ghandi, Hindu Nationalist leader.

"His message has swept Africa. He has done more toward South Africa's future peace than any man." Cecil John Rhodes the Empire Builder.

"Dr John Lake's healing ministry is one of the most remarkable the world has ever seen." Dr William T Gentry, author of Materia Medica, a work of 27 volumes found in almost every medical library.

"The man reveals more of God than any other man in Africa"

Rev. Andrew Murray.

God's creative expression culminates on the sixth day in the making of man in his own image and likeness. This is the day history has been waiting for: the invisible God on exhibit in visible form. Adam stands tall in the stature of his Maker as in a mirror. What God sees satisfies him. Then God sanctifies the seventh day as a celebration of perfection. God's Sabbath continues to celebrate you! God did not 'rest' because he was exhausted; he does not grow weary and does not need a break in order to gather his strength again. Isa 40:26-31. There comes a moment when the artist touches the canvas with a final brush stroke, and signs his name to complete his masterpiece; the reflection of all that his imagination saw, now satisfies him with joy! This is what God's Sabbath celebrates! He invites us to see what he sees in us! In Zephaniah 3:17 this is beautifully portrayed: "He rests in his love, and exults over you with loud singing and exuberant dancing."

Absolutely no work whatsoever is allowed on the Sabbath. More than forty times this commandment is repeated in the Old Testament. Why? What does the Sabbath mean? Imagine inheriting a Van Goch masterpiece and one day feel inspired to add your own touch by mixing some paint and then proceed to add your contribution! You will destroy the original value! You cannot add to pefection.

The Sabbath is God's eternal celebration of his completed work. What God sees in the Sabbath sustains his rest: "And God saw everything that he had made, and behold it was very good." Genesis 1:31. "Ascribe greatness to our God! The Rock; his work is perfect. Is not he your Father who created you, who made you and established you? The Rock that begot you, and the God who gave you birth." Deut 32:3,4,6,18. In the Hebrew the term, "fathered you" in Deut 32:18, kgheel, also has the nuance of "danced with you!" This reminds of the Greek word the early church fathers used to illustrate the relationship of the trinity had with itself...the Perichoresis. Peri = arround, and Choresis = "choreography or Dance". Can you imagine it, Father, Son, and Holy Spirit, circling around each other in a divine dance. In complete unity! The mystery that has been revealed in the Good news is that God himself invited mankind, his highest expression of himself, created in his image and likeness, back into that dance with him. In the Garden we lost our rhythm in the dance but through the incarnation it has been restored for ever more! The dance celebrates perfect union; God's idea of you has always been a friendship of seamless oneness! This is exactly what Jesus redeemed. "I and the Father are one! In that day you will know that I am in my Father and you in me and I in you!" John 10:30 and 14:20.

"When the house was built, it was with stone cut to perfection in the quarry; so that neither hammer nor axe nor any tool of iron was heard in the temple, while it was being built." 1 Kings 6:7. The Quarry in this prophetic picture points to the cross where Jesus cried out, "It is finished!" Mankind's perfection, both by design and redemption is announced in the greatest message ever told! Glad tidings of great joy finds its most articulate voice in Jesus, mirrored in you!

"Every good and perfect gift comes from above; he brought us forth by the word of truth." James 1:17 Without exception God's gifts are only good, its perfection cannot be improved upon. They come [1]from above, *(where we originate from)* proceeding like light rays from its source, the Father of lights. With whom there is no distortion or even a shadow of shifting to obstruct or intercept the light; no hint of a hidden agenda. *(The word, [1]anouthen, means, from above [Jn 3:3, 13]. Man is not the product of his mother's womb; man began in God.)* James 1:18 It was his delightful [1]resolve to give birth to us; we were conceived by the [2]unveiled logic of God. We lead the exhibition of his handiwork, like first fruits introducing the rest of the harvest he anticipates. *(The word, [1]boulomai, means the affectionate desire and deliberate resolve of God. Truth, [2]alethea, from a, negative + lanthano, meaning hidden; that which is unveiled; the word of truth.)*

Nothing that man can do can add to the perfection of God's accomplished work. "You are all together lovely, there is no flaw in you!" Song of Songs 4:7. "From the sole of his feet to the crown of his head, he was without blemish." 2 Sam. 14:25.

Deu 32:3 For I will proclaim the name of the LORD. Ascribe greatness to our God! Deu 32:4 "The Rock, **his work is perfect;** for all his ways are justice. A God of faithfulness and without iniquity, just and right is he. Eph 2:10 We are engineered by his design; he molded and manufactured us in Christ. We are his workmanship, his [1]poetry. *(God finds inspired expression of Christ in us. The Greek word for workmanship is [1]poeima.)* We are [2]fully fit to do good, equipped to give attractive evidence of his likeness in us in everything we do.

Eph 1:3 Let's celebrate God! He lavished every blessing heaven has upon us in Christ! 1:4 He associated us in Christ before [1]the fall of the world! Jesus is God's mind made up about us! He always knew in his love that he would present us again [2]face-to-face before him in blameless innocence. *(The implications of the fall are completely cancelled out. Paul uses the word, [1]katabalo, meaning "to fall away, to put in a lower place," instead of themelios, meaning "foundation" [see 2:20]; thus, translated "the fall of the world," instead of "the foundation of the world," as in most other translations. God found us in Christ before he lost us in Adam! We are presented in blameless innocence before him! The word, [2]katenopion, suggests the closest possible proximity, face-to-face!)*

In sanctifying this special day of rest, God continually extends an opportunity to man to enter into his rest, imploring him to see what he sees. Heb 4:3, Hear the echo of God's [1]cry though the ages, "Oh! If only they would enter into my rest." His rest celebrates perfection. His work is complete; the [2]fall of humanity did not flaw its perfection. He desires for man to discover and embrace the full implication of his finished work. No contribution of man can add any value or virtue to what God has completed; nothing that man can possibly do to change himself or his ways, can add to, change or influence the love and value God already has for mankind! Faith is the ability to see what God sees. Our faith is the value we place upon God's faith in us. God's rest is not at risk. His rest reveals the integrity of his persuasion concerning us. What we already are far exceeds anything we could ever wish to become!

What if man proves to be a total failure; will our unfaithfulness nullify the faithfulness of God? By no means! God remains true and faithful though all men be false! Romans 3:3,4. Man's experience does not prove God right or wrong. "We can do nothing against the truth." 2 Corinthians 13:5,8. If we are faithless, He remains faithful, for he cannot deny himself." 2 Tim 2:13 The Mirror reads, "Our unbelief does not change what God believes; he cannot contradict himself!" *(See Rom 3:3,4 What we believe about God does not define him; God's faith defines us. God cannot be untrue to himself!)*

 Heb 6:11 I urge you to employ that same sincere devotion to now realize the fulfillment of everything that the old system anticipated. Heb 6:12 We do not want you to behave like [1]illegitimate children, unsure of your share in the inheritance. Mimic the faith of those who through their patience came to possess the promise of their allotted portion. *(The word, [1]nothros comes from **nothos**, one born outside of wedlock, of a concubine or female slave. The child of the law and not of the promise. [Gal 3:29]).* Heb 6:13 God could give Abraham no greater guarantee but the integrity of his own being; this makes the promise as sure as God is. 6:14 Saying, "I will continue to speak well of you. I will confirm my intention always only to bless you, and to multiply you beyond measure." *(In blessing I will bless you, and in multiplying I will multiply you.)* 6:15 And so Abraham continued in patience and secured the promise.

Heb 6:16 It is common practice in human affairs to evoke a higher authority under oath in order to add weight to any agreement between men, thereby silencing any possibility of quibbling. *(Putting an end to all dispute.)* Heb 6:17 In the same context we are confronted with God's eagerness to go to the last extreme in his dealing with us as heirs of his promise, and to cancel out all possible grounds for doubt or dispute. In order to persuade us of the unalterable character and finality of his resolve, he confined himself to an oath. The promise which already belongs to us by heritage is now also confirmed under oath. *(The Word is the promise; the Incarnate crucified and risen Christ is the proof. He desires to show more convincingly to the heirs of the promise the unchangeable character of his purpose. — RSV)* Heb 6:18 So that we are now dealing with two irreversible facts *(The promise of redemption sustained throughout scripture and the fulfillment of that promise in Jesus)* which make it impossible for anyone to prove God wrong; thus our persuasion as to our redeemed identity is powerfully reinforced. We have already escaped into that destiny; our expectation has come within our immediate grasp! Heb 6:19 Our hearts and minds are certain; anchored securely within the innermost courts of God's immediate Presence.

It is most liberating to know that God has sworn by himself! He has taken any possible margin for error out of the equation! God was in Christ, reconciling the world to himself! Gal 3:20 With Abraham there was no middleman; it was just God! *(The Mosaic law required mediators because it was an arrangement whereby mankind had a part and God had a part. Mankind's part was to obey the commandments and God's part was to bless. God's covenant with Abraham was a grace covenant; in the man Jesus Christ, God himself would fulfil mankind's part and therefore needed no mediator.)*

Traditional religious rituals like special holy days and festivals, rules and regulations pertaining to fasting and special diets, baptisms, rites and observances, merely held prophetic value until the time and person they pointed towards arrived. Many well meaning Christians are still divided about whether the Sabbath should be held on the first or the seventh day, while the Sabbath is no longer a prophetic promise pointing to the day that would come; the Sabbath has already fully come in the person of Jesus Christ! His finished work on the cross is the eternal celebration of the day of the Lord; the eternal Sabbath has come in him! Who Jesus is and what he has done reflect all that God sees in the Sabbath!

2 Tim 1:9 He rescued the [1]integrity of our original [2]design and revealed that we have always been his own from the beginning, even [3]before time was. This has nothing to do with anything we did to qualify or disqualify ourselves. We are not talking religious good works or karma here. Jesus unveils grace to be the [4]eternal intent of God! Grace celebrates our pre-creation innocence and now declares our redeemed union with God in Christ Jesus. *([1]hagios, holiness, purity, integrity kaleo, often translated, holy calling; [2]kaleo means to identify by name, to surname; [3]pro xronos aionos; pro, before; xronos, a specific space or portion of time, season; aionios, without beginning or end, timeless perpetuity, ages; this was before calendar time existed, before the creation of the galaxies and constellations. There exists a greater dimension to eternity than what we are capable of defining within the confines of space and time! God's faith anticipated the exact moment of our redeemed union with him*

for all eternity! What happened to us in Christ is according to God's eternal purpose (⁴prothesis), which he has shown in every prophetic pointer and shadow; in the Hebrew tradition the showbread (prothesis) pointed to the true bread from heaven, the authentic word that proceeded from the mouth of God, Jesus the incarnate word sustaining the life of our design. See Heb 9:2 The first tented area was called the Holy Place; the only light here came from the lamp-stand illuminating the table upon which the showbread (prosthesis) was presented, (the lamp-stand was a beautifully crafted golden chandelier portraying budding and blossoming almond branches. Remember that this is also what Jeremiah saw in Jer 1:12, when God said, 'I am awake over my word to perform it.' The same Hebrew word is used here, shaqad, the almond was called the 'awake tree', because it blossomed first, while the other trees were still in their winter sleep. The show bread pointed towards the daily sustenance of life in the flesh as the ultimate tabernacle of God, realized in the account of Jesus with the two men from Emmaus; their hearts were burning with resonance and faith while he opened the scriptures to them, and then around the table their eyes were opened to recognize him as the fulfillment of scripture, their true meal incarnated: Luke 24:27-31; Man shall not live by bread alone, but by the authentic thought of God, the Word proceeding from his mouth, the original intent, his image and likeness incarnated, revealed and redeemed in human life.)

Titus 1:2 This is the life of the ages that was anticipated for generations; the life of our original design announced by the infallible resolve of God before time or space existed. (Man's union with God is the original thought that inspired creation. aionios, without beginning or end, timeless perpetuity, ages; xronos, a specific space or portion of time, season. This was before calendar time existed, before the creation of the galaxies and constellations. There exists a greater dimension to eternity than what we are capable of defining within the confines of space and time! God's faith anticipated the exact moment of our redeemed union with him for all eternity! *Mirror Bible*

This life was made certain before eternal time. *(BBE 1949, Bible in Basic English)*

Titus 1:3 My message announces the completeness of time; God's eternal moment realized the logic of our salvation. *(But then the day dawned; the most complete culmination of time! [Gal 4:4] Everything predicted was concluded in Christ!)*

We celebrate an innocence that pre-dates Adam's fall! We have allowed an illegitimate sin-consciousness to prevail in our theologies and worship! The prodigal son's Father had no reference or remembrance of past sins; imagine how that would spoil the party! (Note on 2 Tim 1:3 Mirror) Col 2:8 Make sure that you become no one's victim through empty philosophical intellectualism and meaningless speculations, molded in traditions and repetitions according to man's cosmic codes and superstitions and not consistent with Christ. *(Any teaching that leaves you with a sense of lack and imperfection rather than completeness is a distraction from the truth.)*

Col 2:9 Christ reveals that there is no place in the universe where God would rather be; the fullness of Deity physically resides in him! Jesus proves that human life is tailor-made for God! *(While the expanse cannot measure or define God, his exact likeness is displayed in human form. The human body frames the most complete space for Deity to dwell in!)*

Col 2:10 Jesus mirrors our completeness and ¹endorses our ²true identity. He is "I am" in us. *(Isn't it amazing that God packaged completeness in "I am," mirrored in you! Delay is outdated! The word, ¹**arche**, means chief in rank. The word, ²**exousia**, means authority from **ek + eimi**, originating out of "I am." The days are over where our lives were dictated to under the rule of the law of performance and an inferior identity. [See Col 1:19] The full measure of everything God has in mind for man indwells him.*

"Your own completeness is only realized in him." — Phillips Translation.)

Col 2:11 You were in Christ when he died which means that his death represents your true circumcision. Sin's authority in the human body was stripped off you in him dying your death.

Col 2:12 In the same parallel *(your co-circumcision in his death)* your co-burial and joint-resurrection is now demonstrated in baptism; your co-inclusion in Christ is what God's faith knew when he powerfully raised him from the dead. *(Hos 6:2)*

Col 2:13 You were once spiritually dead, as confirmed in your constant failure; being bound to a lifestyle ruled by the ¹distorted desires of the flesh, but now God has made you alive together with him, having forgiven you all your ²trespasses. *(¹The uncircumcision of the flesh, i.e., in the Greek, a life controlled by the sexual organs. The word, ²**paraptoma**, comes from, **para**, close proximity, sphere of influence and **pipto**, to stop flying, from **petomai**, to fly; thus, to fall from flight or to lose altitude.)*

Col 2:14 His body nailed to the cross hung there as the document of mankind's guilt; in dying our death he ¹deleted the detailed ²hand-written ³record of Adam's fall. Every ¹stain that sin left on our conscience was fully blotted out. *(The word, ¹**exaleipho**, comes from **ek**, out of, and **aleipho**, with **a**, as a particle of union, and **liparos**, to grease, to leave a stain; guilt was like a grease stain upon the conscience of fallen man. The word, ²**cheirographon**, translates as hand-written. The word, ³**dogma**, comes from **dokeo**, a thought pattern; thus thought patterns engraved by human experience of constant failure to do what the law required. In his personal handwriting man endorsed his own death sentence.*

The hands of fallen man struck the body of Jesus with the blows of their religious hatred and fury when they nailed his bloodied body to the tree; they did not realize that in the mystery of God's economy Jesus was the scapegoat of the entire human race! [Isa 53:4, 5] "The slate wiped clean, that old arrest warrant canceled and nailed to Christ's Cross." — The Message)

Col 2:15 His brilliant victory made a public [1]spectacle of every [2]rule and [3]authority empowered by the fall of Adam. The [4]voice of the cross will never be silenced! *(The horror of the Cross is now the eternal trophy of God's triumph over sin! The cross stripped religion of its authority to manipulate man with guilt. Every accusation lost its power to continue to blackmail the human race. The word, [1]apekduomai, is translated from apo, away from, and ekduo, to be stripped of clothing; the religious facade that disguised the law of works as a means of defining man was openly defeated. The dominance of the tree of the knowledge of good and evil (poneros, hard work and labor) was ended. The word, [1]deikmatizo, means to exhibit in public. The word, [4]parresia, comes from pas, all and rheo, outspokenness, pouring forth speech.*

"He stripped all the spiritual tyrants in the universe of their sham authority at the Cross and marched them naked through the streets." — The Message

See commentary for 1 Corinthians 15:24, The complete conclusion in his work of redemption is celebrated in his yielding the full harvest of his reign to God the Father, having [1]brought to naught the law of works which supported every definition of dominion under the fall, including all [2]principalities, all [3]authority and every [4]dynamic influence in society. [He brought to naught the law of works, [1]katargeo, from kata, meaning intensity, and argos, meaning labor; thus free from all self effort to attempt to improve what God has already perfected in Christ. All principalities, [2]arche, or chief ranks, i.e., kings, governors; this includes any governing system whereby one is ranked above the other on the basis of their performance or preference. All authority, [3]exousia, comes from ek, denoting origin and eimi, I am; in this case, because of what I can do I am defined by what I can do better than you; therefore, I have authority over you. Every dynamic influence in society, [4]dunamis, means power, in this case, willpower. Every government structure in society will be brought under the dominion of grace where the Christ life rules.]

In 1 Corinthians 2:7-8, We voice words of wisdom that was hidden in silence for timeless ages; a mystery unfolding God's Masterful plan whereby he would redeem his glory in man. Neither the politicians nor the theologians of the day had a clue about this mystery [of mankind's association in Christ]; if they did, they would never have crucified the Lord whose death redeemed our glory!)

Col 2:16 Do not let anyone therefore bring a restriction to your freedom by reviving religious rules and regulations pertaining to eating and drinking; all Jewish festivals, new moons, and Sabbaths have come to an end in Christ! *(Their relevance only served to remind of the promise of Christ on an annual, monthly, and weekly basis. They carried the promise like a placenta would hold the unborn child, but became obsolete as soon as the child was born.)*

Col 2:17 These things were only prophetic shadows; Christ is the substance.

Col 2:18 A religious mentality of voluntary humility and obsession with pious observances of angels will bring you no further reward. So do not let anyone who tries to act as an umpire of your devotion insist on his own opinion, confined to a mind inflated by the sensational and spooky; his so called visions are just a puff of hot air. *(In his judgment he fails to correctly interpret the legal implications of the Cross.)*

"Don't tolerate people who try to run your life, ordering you to bow and scrape, [in order to improve your standing before God], insisting that you join their obsession with angels and that you seek out visions. They're a lot of hot air, that's all they are." — The Message.

Col 2:19 Such religious jargon is completely out of rhythm with the head. You are directly connected to Christ who like a ¹choir conductor draws out the music in everyone like a tapestry of art that intertwines in harmony to reveal the full stature of divine inspiration. *(Which is Christ in you. The word, ¹epichoregeo, is choir director. [See 2 Pet 1:11] Thus, the great Conductor of music will draw your life into the full volume of the harmony of the ages.)*

Col 2:20 If it is true that you were included in Christ's death, then the religious systems of this world with its rules and regulations no longer apply to you. What further relevance would there be for you to continue to live under the influence of man's doctrines and ideas?

Col 2:21 Things like: "Do not associate with this one!" or "Do not taste that!" or "Do not even touch this with your finger!"

Col 2:22 These instructions are of no permanent value in any case since they refer to things that perish after it is consumed, thus they leave no lasting impact in your life. So do not let man's menus cause you to major on minors. *(Jesus said it is not what goes into the mouth that matters, but what comes out of the heart!)*

Col 2:23 Religious tradition appears to be very devout and its followers seem to be so humble and holy in their strict observance of rules that seek to control the behavior of the body. The only problem with this is that the flesh is never permanently satisfied. *(The Message translates verses 19-23 as: "They're completely out of touch with the source of life, Christ, who puts us together in one piece, whose very breath and blood flow through us. He is the Head and we are the body. We can grow up healthy in God only as he nourishes us. So, then, if with Christ you've put all that pretentious and infantile religion behind you, why do you let yourselves be bullied by it? "Don't touch this! Don't taste that! Don't go near this!" Do you think things that are here today and gone tomorrow are worth that kind of attention? Such things sound impressive if said in a deep enough voice. They even give the illusion of being pious and humble and ascetic.)* The Mirror

It is clear that the Sabbath was fulfilled in Christ; we are no longer celebrating a day, but a life! The prophetic word is like a placenta that held the unborn child. Now the child deserves all the attention.

God invites us to enter into his Rest on the same basis that he enjoys Rest. Our best attempts to rest can never match his! He encourages us to see what he sees, to walk in the light as he is in the light. We are to see ourselves as he sees us, exclusively. Mankind could neither create nor redeem themselves. "All this is from God." 2 Co 5:18. Of God's doing are we in Christ. 1 Cor. 1:30. He is the Alpha and the Omega. Rev.1:8. Personal achievement through religious devotion and discipline cannot influence the love and favour of God. It is futile to seek to obtain something you already have! No need to try and win God's attention if you already have it! He has always known you and has always only loved you! Jesus is proof that you matter to your Maker more than anything else! The essence of the revelation of the Gospel is the fact that God is well pleased with man. This is a non-negotiable. Nothing can separate man from the love of God!

"Before Abraham was, I am!" John 8:58. God's time is an eternal concept; hence the scriptures refer to the Lamb of God that was slain before the fall of the human race. Revelation 13:8. *(Greek: kataballo, to be cast down, this refers to the fall of man.)* Jesus is the fullness of time. God found us in Christ before he lost us in Adam. Faith is God's language; he calls things that are not yet visible as though they were! Rom 4:17.

The angels announced the good pleasure and favor of God at the birth of Jesus and echoed the prophetic word before anyone responded to God's love initiative.

Eph 2:7 God is now able for timeless perpetuity *(the eternal future)* to exhibit the trophy of the wealth of his grace demonstrated in his kindness towards us in Christ Jesus. Grace exhibits excessive evidence of the success of the cross.

Eph 2:8 Your salvation is not a reward for good behavior! It was a grace thing from start to finish; you had no hand in it. Even the gift to believe simply reflects his faith! *(You did not invent faith; it was God's faith to begin with! It is from faith to faith, [Rom 1:17] He is both the source and conclusion of faith. [Heb 12:2])*

Eph 2:9 If this could be accomplished through any action of yours then there would be ground for boasting.

Eph 2:10 We are engineered by his design; he molded and manufactured us in Christ. We are his workmanship, his [1]poetry. *(God finds inspired expression of Christ in us. The Greek word for workmanship is [1]poeima.)* We are [2]fully fit to do good, equipped to give attractive evidence of his likeness in us in everything we do. *(God has done everything possible to find spontaneous and effortless expression of his character in us in our everyday lifestyle. The word, [2]proetoimatso, translates a notion that God has prepared a highway for us to lead us out like kings, just like the Oriental custom, where people would go before a king to level the roads to make it possible for the king to journey with ease and comfort. [Isa 40:3-5])*

Rom 2:4 Do not [1]underestimate God's [2]kindness. The wealth of his [2]benevolence and his [3]resolute refusal to let go of us in his [4]patient passion is to [5]shepherd everyone into a [6]radical mind shift. *(The word translated, underestimate is the word, [1]kataphroneō, from kata, down, and phroneo, to think, to form an opinion; thus a downcast mind, to despise or take for granted. It is the revelation of the goodness of God that leads us to [6]repentance; it is not our "repentance" that leads God to goodness! The word "repentance" is a fabricated word from the Latin word, penance, and to give religion more mileage the English word became re-penance! This is not what the Greek word means at all! The word, [6]metanoia, comes from meta, meaning together with, and nous, mind; thus, together with God's mind. This word suggests a [6]radical mind shift; it is to realize God's thoughts towards us. [See Isa 55:8-10] The word, [2]chrestos, kind, benevolent, from xeir, hand which is also root to the word xristos, to draw the hand over, to annoint, to measure; see also the Hebrew for Messiah, mashach, to draw the hand over, to measure! [Analytical Hebrew and Chaldee Lexicon, B Davidson.] In Jesus Christ God has measured mankind innocent, he is the blueprint of our design! The word [3]anoches comes from ana, meaning upwards; ana also shows intensity and the word echo, to hold, or embrace, as in echo. He continues to hear the echo of his likeness in us! [See Rom 3:26.] The word, [4]makrothumias, means to be patient in bearing the offenses and injuries of others. Literally, passion that goes a long way; from the root word thuo, to slay a sacrifice. The word, [5]ago, means to lead as a shepherd leads his sheep.)*

Rom 4:4 There is a large difference between a reward and a gift: if you have earned something through hard work; what you receive in return is your due and certainly not a gift.

We are the fruit of the travail of his soul. Is. 53:11. We are his reward, he is our gift.

Eph 4:7 The gift of Christ gives dimension to grace and defines our individual value. *(Grace was given to each one of us according to the measure of the gift of Christ. One measure, one worth! Our worth is defined by his gift not by a reward for our behavior.)*

Eph 4:8 Scripture confirms that he led us as trophies in his triumphant procession on high; he [1]repossessed his gift *(likeness)* in man. *(See Ephesians 2:6, We are also elevated in his ascension to be equally welcome in the throne room of the heavenly realm where we are now seated together with him in his authority. Quote from the Hebrew text, Ps 68:18, [1]lakachta mattanoth baadam, thou hast taken gifts in man, in Adam. [The gifts which Jesus Christ distributes to man he has received in man, in and by virtue of his incarnation. Commentary by Adam Clarke.] We were born anew in his resurrection. 1 Pet 1:3, Hos 6:2)*

Eph 4:9 The fact that he ascended confirms his victorious descent into the deepest pits of human despair. *(See John 3:13, "No one has ascended into heaven but he who [1]descended from heaven, even the son of man." All mankind originate from above; we are [1]anouthen, from above [see Jas 1:17, 18].)*

Eph 4:10 He now occupies the ultimate rank of authority from the lowest regions where he stooped down to rescue us to the highest authority in the heavens, having executed his mission to the full. *(Fallen man is fully restored to the authority of the authentic life of his design. [Ps 139:8].)*

Eph 4:11 What God has in us is gift wrapped to the world.

Rom 3:27 The law of faith cancels the law of works; which means there is suddenly nothing left for man to boast in. No one is superior to another. *(Bragging only makes sense if there is someone to compete with or impress. "While we compete with one another and compare ourselves with one another we are without understanding. [2 Cor 10:12]. "Through the righteousness of God we have received a faith of equal standing." [See 2 Pet 1:1 RSV] The OS (operating system) of the law of works is willpower; the OS of the law of faith is love. Gal 5:6 Love sets faith in motion. The law presented man with choices; grace awakens belief! Willpower exhausts, love ignites! If choices could save us we would be our own Saviors! Willpower is the language of the law, love is the language of grace and it ignites faith that leads to romance; falling in love beats "making a decision to believe in love"! See Rom 7:19)*

"In returning and rest you shall be saved; in quietness and in trust shall be your strength." Isaiah 30:15.

The Sabbath means to see and celebrate with God. It is an eternal festival of gratitude, a celebration of perfection.

GOOD WORKS

Where do good works fit into the picture? We have seen in the previous chapter that our own good works cannot save us; neither can it influence God in any way to love and accept us more than what he already does. God does not love people differently; he desires all men to be saved and to come to the knowledge of the truth. 1 Timothy 2:4. "For God so loved the world, that he gave Jesus; he did not come to condemn the world, but to save the world." John 3:16,17. "For the love of God constrains us, because we are convinced that one died for all, therefore all have died. God was in Christ, reconciling the world to himself." 2 Corinthians 5:14,19. Can a woman forget her nursing child? This is the strongest bond that exists in human relationships. As unlikely as this seems, it may be possible, but I can never forget you; I have tattooed your name upon the palms of my hand!" Isaiah 49:15,16.

Titus 3:5 Salvation is not a reward for good behavior. It has absolutely nothing to do with anything that we have done. God's mercy saved us. The Holy Spirit endorses in us what happened to us when Jesus Christ died and was raised! When we heard the glad announcement of salvation it was like taking a deep warm bath! We were thoroughly cleansed and resurrected in a new birth! It was a complete renovation that restored us to sparkling newness of life! *(We realized that we were indeed co-included, co-crucified, and co-raised and are now co-seated together with Christ in heavenly places! [See 2 Cor 5:14-21; Hosea 6:2; Eph 2:5, 6; and 1 Pet 1:3])*

Eph 2:10 We are engineered by his design; he molded and manufactured us in Christ. We are his workmanship, his [1]poetry. *(God finds inspired expression of Christ in us. The Greek word for workmanship is [1]**poeima**.)* We are fully fit to do good, equipped to give attractive evidence of his likeness in us in everything we do. *(God has done everything possible to find spontaneous and effortless expression of his character in us in our everyday lifestyle.*

Gal 5:13 Your redeemed identity defines your freedom, my brothers! But freedom does not mean that you are now free to again employ the law. On the contrary, your freedom finds its most complete expression in a love that serves one another! As free as you are to the law, so enslaved you are now to love! *(You are at last free to live the life of your original design.)*

Gal 5:22 The Spirit finds expression in love, joy, peace, endurance, kindness *(usefulness, obliging)*, goodness, faith, gentleness, self control *(spirit strength)*.

(In total contrast to the tree of the knowledge of good and evil, the tree of life bears fruit effortlessly consistent with the life of our original design!)

Gal 5:23 Legalism can neither match nor contradict this. There is no law against love! *(Love does not compete with law; love is extravagant in its exhibition of the Christ life.)*

Rom 13:9 Love makes it impossible for you to commit adultery, or to kill someone, or to steal from someone, speak evil of anyone, or to covet anything that belongs to someone else. Your only option is to esteem a fellow human with equal value to yourself.

Rom 13:10 Everything love does is to the advantage of another; therefore, love is the most complete expression of what the law requires.

A true artist paints by inspiration not by duty; love exceeds law.

Good works are the spontaneous and dynamic consequence of our redeemed identity and innocence realized: "For the fruit of the spirit is goodness." Galatians 5:22. When Paul speaks about the fruit of the spirit he is referring to the fruit of righteousness by faith vs. selfrighteousness by the law of works and performance.

"Love your enemies; bless them that curse you, do good to them that hate you, and pray for them who despitefully abuse you, and persecute you; that you may display your father's character; he makes his sun shine on the evil and on the good, and sends rain on the just as well as the unjust." Mathew 5:44,45. "The fruit of the spirit is in all goodness and righteousness and truth." Ephesians 5:9. "Let your light so shine before men, that they may see your good works and glorify your Father." Good works reveal the glory and opinion of the Father. (The word often translated as glory, is the Greek word, *doxa,* from *dokeo* which means to form an opinion, suggesting the intenet of God. Our good works demonstrate to people how God sees them. "He is the father of the orphan, and the protector of the widow. God gives the desolate a home to dwell in; he leads out the prisoners into prosperity." Psalm 68:5,6. "This is the essence of true religion: to visit the widow and orphan in their affliction." James 1:27. God is attracted to the lonely.

"What must we do, to be doing the works of God? Jesus answered them: This is the work of God: that you believe in him whom he has sent." John 6:28. This means to see in Christ what God sees in him. He is not an example for us, but of us! "Truly, truly, I say unto you, whoever believes in me will also do the works that I do; and greater works than these will he do, because I go to the Father. Whatever you ask in my Name, I will do it, that the Father may be glorified in the son; if you ask anything in my Name, I will do it." John 14:12-14.

"Why do you spend your money for that which is not bread and labour for that which does not satisfy?" Is. 55:2.

James 2:14 My brothers, if your faith *(in your true identity)* is not practical and visible in your conduct it is fake and cannot benefit you in any way.

James 2:15 Let's bring it closer to home *(I am not even talking about your duty to strangers)*, someone in your own family might be struggling financially to the extent that they do not even have the basics as far as clothes and food are concerned.

James 2:16 What's the good if you keep your contact with them very brief and distant and wave them goodbye with empty words, something like, "May the Lord richly bless you brother! Be warm, be fed, ok, bye! Have a great day!" A coat and a cup of soup is going to say so much more!

James 2:17 It is clear then that without corresponding acts of kindness, faith on its own is fake.

James 2:18 Faith is not in competition with works; the one cannot operate without the other. Faith remains invisible without action; indeed the only way to communicate faith is in doing the things prompted and inspired by faith.

When Jesus saw the crowd, he had compassion on them, and he taught them and healed their sick. And great crowds came to him, bringing with them, not their broken chairs and tables for the carpenter to repair, but the lame, the maimed, the blind, the dumb, and many others, and they put them at his feet, and he healed them. Then Jesus called his disciples and said to them: I have compassion on the crowd, because they have been with me now three days, and have nothing to eat; and I am unwilling to send them away hungry, lest they faint on the way. But the disciples said, "Where will we get enough bread in the wilderness to feed such a large crowd?" A valid response, one would argue, yet Jesus was about to reveal to them that there exists a realm of supply and supernatural provision closer to us than the nearest Supermarket and exceeding our budget. "Give them what you have." He said. God has called us into a divine partnership where he turns our situation of apparent need and lack into a new dimension, exceedingly, abundantly, above all that we could ask for, or even imagine! Mathew 14:14-21, 15:30-38. Ephesians 3:20. It was not the five-loaves-and-two-fish-formula that did the trick, it was a new economy of love's provision that transforms the impossible into abundance.

"And Jesus went about all the cities and villages, teaching in their synagogues and preaching the gospel of the kingdom, and healing every disease and every infirmity. When he saw the crowds, he had compassion for them, for they were harassed and exploited, like sheep without a shepherd, at the mercy of the wolves." (In Psalm 105:37 we see such a different picture: when Israel was rescued out of Egypt, there was not a feeble person among them; now, many years later, they are worse off in Canaan and the established religious structures than what they were in the wilderness!) Then he said to his disciples, "The harvest is plentiful, but the labourers are few, pray the Lord of the harvest to send out labourers into his harvest." "And he called to him his twelve disciples and gave them authority over unclean spirits, to cast them out, and to heal every disease and every infirmity." Math.9:35-10:1. "Thereafter he appointed another seventy, and sent them on ahead, two by two into the cities where he himself was about to come." Luke 10:1.

Prior to his ascension, Jesus told his disciples, a hundred and twenty at that time, to wait in Jerusalem for the Promise of the Father, until they are clothed with power from on high. Luke 24:49. "And you shall receive power when the Holy Spirit has come upon you; and you shall be my witnesses, locally, nationally and globally." Acts 1:8.

1 Cor 3:4 Can you not see that it is not about Paul or Apollos or any teacher you wish to associate with? We are not here to play the one off against the other, in a desperate attempt to win your vote to join our "group." *(Acts 19:1)*

1 Cor 3:5 Both Apollos and I are on the same assignment: we are here for you, to influence your faith to discover yourself in Christ. Every individual is equally gifted in him. *(See verses 21 and 22)*

1 Cor 3:6 I have planted, by bringing the gospel to you in the first place, then Apollos watered the seed in his ministry to you; but God causes the Christ life to ignite and expand in you.

1 Cor 3:7 If all we succeeded to do was to attach you to us as individuals, then we have failed you; the one who plants is not more important than the one who waters; it is not about us, it is about you realizing God's work within you. *(Our ministry has only one objective: to reveal Christ in you! See Paul's urgency in Philemon 2:12, "not only in my presence but much more in my absence, discover the full extent of your own salvation: it is God working in you both to will and to do!" This "working out your own salvation" has nothing in common with the duty driven, willpower-restricted law of works system. It is discovering his working in you; energizing you with both the desire and capacity to give expression to him.)*

1 Cor 3:8 Our individual assignment does not place the one above the other; we have exactly the same mission; how we succeed or fail in that is to our own account.

1 Cor 3:9 We are co-employed by God. You are God's agricultural field; or in another context, you are his building and he is the architect and engineer of the life of your design.

1 Cor 3:10 His grace is the only reference to my skill; his gift qualifies me *(I did not earn my certificate as Master Builder at a university as a reward to my excellence!)*. The faith foundation that I have laid in your lives gives evidence to that. So let the next man take extra caution to build consistent with what grace communicates. *(Grace alone defines and inspires New Testament ministry.)*

1 Cor 3:11 Jesus Christ is the only foundation; nothing that anyone else can possibly teach you can replace him.

1 Cor 3:12 Imagine the contrast in building materials, one builds with gold, silver and precious stones, while another uses wood, hay and stubble. *(By comparison, the teaching of the cross and its glorious effect in the believer's life is like building with gold, silver, and precious stones, whereas the wisdom of this world system based upon religious good works and not faith is like building with wood, hay, and stubble which is fuel for fire!)*

1 Cor 3:13 Everyone's work shall be tested in the scrutiny of real life; it shall be made apparent as in broad daylight just as gold is tested in fire: what you teach will either burn like stubble or shine like gold. *(The revelation of man's co-crucifixion and co-resurrection with Christ is the gold of the gospel!)*

1 Cor 3:14 If what you teach is based on the revelation of the success of the cross it will certainly be confirmed in the heat of contradiction.

1 Cor 3:15 Obviously to witness the fruit of your labor go up in smoke would be devastating to anyone, even though you escape with your own life!

1 Cor 3:16 Realize that your life is God's building; his sanctuary, designed for his permanent abode. His Spirit inhabits you! *(He designed every cell in your body to accommodate and express him.)*

Paul's Passion: *"I am not for sale; I am employed by the economy of persuasion!"*

1 Cor 9:7 Imagine a soldier goes to war at his own expense! I mean how absurd! Yet it is almost taken for granted that Barnabas and I have to earn our own living not to burden the very people we established and daily feed in their faith!

1 Cor 9:8 Anyone who plants a vineyard eats its fruit for free; the shepherd likewise is not expected to pay for a drink of milk!

1 Cor 9:9 Or is this just my own idea? If you insist on scriptural evidence, even the law of Moses says that the ox treading out the grain shall not be muzzled!

1 Cor 9:10 If God so cares for the oxen imagine how much more he cares for you! Moses certainly had more than oxen in mind in writing this; the farmer would be wasting his time plowing his field without participating in the harvest. While the oxen were still treading out the corn the farmer joyfully anticipates the bread.

1 Cor 9:11 Spiritual seed also translates into a material harvest.

1 Cor 9:12 While others enjoy this privilege why would it seem wrong that we share the same? We have not taken any advantage of you; we would rather suffer lack than insisting on our rights and in the process cause you to be distracted from the gospel of Christ.

1 Cor 9:13 It is common knowledge that the people engaged in temple ministry eat what is sacrificed there.

1 Cor 9:14 The same principle goes for those who proclaim the Gospel; and this is not just someone's good idea it is endorsed by the Lord.

1 Cor 9:15 The reason for my writing about these issues is not to bring you under any kind of obligation; on the contrary, I want to be very clear about this, the fact that I do things differently by not expecting anyone to pay me for my ministry is to emphasize my urgency to remove any possible excuse from anyone's mind that I might have ulterior motives! I am dead serious about this Gospel!

1 Cor 9:16 I live to preach; it consumes my total being. Your money is not going to make any difference since this Gospel has my arm twisted and locked behind my back! (anagke) In fact, my life would be reduced to utter misery if it were not possible for me to preach the good news!

1 Cor 9:17 If this was a mere career choice, then surely you could hire or fire me! But I am not for sale; I am employed by the economy of persuasion!

1 Cor 9:18 So what's in it for me? You may ask! The pleasure of declaring the Gospel of Christ at no expense is priceless! No, I am not cheating anyone or myself by foregoing the rights I might have as a preacher.

1 Cor 9:19 So in a sense I am free from anyone's expectation or management; yet I have voluntarily enslaved myself to all people. This beats any other motivation to influence people.

1 Cor 9:20 I am like a Jew to the Jew to win them; I am disguised as a legalist to win those stuck under the law!

1 Cor 9:21 To the Gentiles who have no regard for Jewish sentiment, I became like one without any obligation to Jewish laws; to win them! Don't get me wrong; I am not sinning to identify with the sinners! I am in the law of Christ! *(The agape law!)*

1 Cor 9:22 I am so persuaded about every person's inclusion in Christ that I desire to be everything I need to be in order to win everyone's understanding of their union with Christ. I do not present myself as super strong to the weak, but would expose myself to their weakness in order to win them. I do not distance myself from anyone. My mission is to be exactly what is required of me in every possible situation to bring salvation to [1]every kind of person, whoever they are! *(Traditionally translated, "in order to save some;" this is not what Paul is saying! In the Greek, [1]tis, suggests every single kind.)*

1 Cor 9:23 The gospel explains my lifestyle; it is so much more than a pulpit ministry to me. My life is inseparably joined to you in the fellowship of the good news!

1 Cor 9:24 An athlete runs a race to win; his aim is to receive the prize not just to compete! This why I preach, to persuade you and not just to entertain you! *(A soccer player can do magic with his footwork and soccer ball skills, but it is no good if he cannot take the gap and score the goal!)*

1 Cor 9:25 The athlete knows how to draw from focused inner strength in order to win the crown; for them all their effort translates into a mere moment celebrated by a fading wreath of honor. For us to win your faith is of imperishable value!

1 Cor 9:26 I run with certain victory in my every step! I am not shadow boxing when I preach!

1 Cor 9:27 I deliberately compare myself to the sacrifice and dedication of a champion athlete; in similar fashion I would pommel my body and subdue it! I would deny myself many things in my pursuit to win your faith so that you will not have any excuse to reject my message. I want you, not your money! *(Paul is not saying this because he is worried about God's approval. It is his audience's approval that he is after: "becoming all things to all types of people in order to win every single one of them!" 1 Corinthians 9:12, we would rather suffer lack than insisting on our rights and in the process cause you to be distracted from the gospel of Christ. [See also Paul's urgency in Col 1:25-28])*

Compare the difference in these translations! "For we must all appear before the judgement seat of Christ, so that each one may receive according to what he has done in the body." 2 Corinthians 5:10 If this is what Paul said then we better run from God, cause he's gonna get you!

Now hear the Mirror translation! 2 Cor 5:10 For we have all been [1]thoroughly scrutinized in the [2]footsteps of Jesus; *(not as an example for us but of us)* and are [3]taken care of and restored to the life of our design, regardless of what happened to us in our individual lives, whatever amazing or meaningless things that we encountered in the body. *(The word, [1]phaneroo, means to render apparent, to openly declare, to manifest. Paul uses the aorist passive infinitive tense **phanerothenai**, not referring to a future event. The aorist tense is like a snapshot taken of an event that is already concluded. The word, **bematos**, comes from [2]**bayma**, means footprint, also referring to a raised place mounted by steps, or a tribunal, the official seat of a judge The word, [3]**komitzo**, comes from **kolumbos**, meaning to tend, to take care of, to provide for, to carry off from harm. Paul's reference was not how much abuse and affliction he suffered, neither was it the many good times he remembered that defined him; "I am what I am by the grace of God!" If we are still to be judged for good or bad deeds that we performed in the body, then the judgment that Jesus faced on humanity's behalf seems irrelevant.)*

2 Cor 5:11 We persuade people in the [1]radiance of the Lord! His visible glory is mirrored in us! Our lives are transparent before God; we anticipate that you will witness the same transparency in your [2]conscience! *(The word, [1]**suneido**, translates as conscience, joint seeing. In 2 Corinthians 4:2, "with the open statement of the truth we commend ourselves to everyone's conscience." The word, **phobe**, speaks of dread terror and fear! I would prefer to use the word, [1]**phoibe**, which means radiant! Now that sounds more typical of the God of creation who unveiled himself in Christ! Jesus is the express image of God, the radiance of his beauty! He has made the invisible God visible! He is the Father of lights with whom there is no shadow due to compromise; there is no dark side to God! To persuade people with fear is in total contradiction to what Paul's ministry was all about! See in verse 14, the love of Christ persuades me that one has died for all; this can only mean that all in fact were equally included in his death!)*

2 Cor 5:12 We do not want you to pity us, but rather to be proud of us for your own sakes! We are not into window-dressing because we are not into window-shopping. Neither are we here to impress you with us but to impress you with you!

2 Cor 5:13 We are [1]blissfully out of our minds with pleasure before our Maker; he delights in our ecstasy. Our insane mode is between us and God; we promise to behave ourselves sane and sober before you! *(The word, [1]**ekstase**, is to be blissfully out of one's mind with pleasure!)*

2 Cor 5:14 The love of Christ [1]resonates within us and leaves us with only

one conclusion: Jesus died humanity's death; therefore, in God's logic every individual simultaneously died. *(The word, [1]sunecho, from sun, meaning together with and echo, meaning to echo, to embrace, to hold, and thus translated, to resonate. Jesus didn't die 99% or for 99%. He died humanity's death 100%! If Paul had to compromise the last part of verse 14 to read: "one died for all therefore only those who follow the prescriptions to qualify, have also died," then he would have had to change the first half of the verse as well! Only the love of Christ can make a calculation of such enormous proportion! Theology would question the extremity of God's love and perhaps prefer to add a condition or two to a statement like that!)*

Col 1:24 This is why no form of suffering can interfere with my joy. Every suffering on your behalf is just another opportunity to reinforce that which might still be lacking *(in your understanding)* of the affliction of Christ on behalf of his body which is the church. *(The inconvenience that Paul might be suffering on behalf of the believers is not to add to the sufferings of Christ—as though the sufferings of Christ on our behalf were insufficient but it is to further emphasize and confirm the principle of unselfish love that constrains New Testament ministry.)*

Col 1:25 I am an administrator in God's economy; my mission is to make his word known to you with utmost clarity.

Col 1:26 The element of prophetic mystery was concealed for ages and generations but is now fully realized in our redeemed innocence.

Col 1:27 In us God desires to exhibit the priceless treasure of Christ's indwelling; every nation will recognize him as in a mirror! The unveiling of Christ in human life completes man's every expectation. *(He is not hiding in history, or in outer space nor in the future, neither in the pages of scripture, he is merely mirrored there to be unveiled within you. Mt 13:44, Gal 1:15, 16)*

Col 1:28 This is the essence and focus of our message; we [1]awaken every man's mind, instructing every individual by bringing them into [2]full understanding *(flawless clarity)* in order that we may [3]prove *(present)* everyone [4]perfect in Christ. *(Translating [1]vous + tithemi as to re-align every mind with God's mind. The word, [2]sophos, comes from sophes meaning clear, clarity. The word, [3]paristano, comes from para, sphere of influence, closest possible association, and histemi, meaning to stand, to exhibit with evidence. The word, [4]teleios, means perfect, without shortcoming and fully efficient.)*

Col 1:29 [1]Your completeness in Christ is my point of departure! My labor now exceeds any zeal that I previously knew under the law of willpower and duty. I am laboring beyond the point of exhaustion, striving with intense resolve with all the energy that he mightily inspires within me. *([1]eis, a point reached in conclusion.)*

2 Tim 1:10 Everything that grace pointed to is now realized in Jesus Christ and brought into clear view through the gospel: Jesus is what grace reveals. He took death out of the equation and re-defines life; this is good news indeed!

2 Tim 1:11 Grace is my commission; it is my job and joy to proclaim this message and guide the nations into a full understanding of the love initiative of God.

2 Tim 1:12 What I suffer because of this does not frighten me at all; faith has made him so [1]apparent. I am absolutely persuaded that I am safe in him. We are no longer looking for a future event, or another day, the day has come! Death is not doomsday; nothing can interrupt what he has done! *(Greek, [1]eido, Latin, video, to see, to know)*

2 Tim 2:9 I might be in bonds, but the Word of God is not. *(It might seem to some that my suffering contradicts what I preach, but it cannot! My ministry is measured by the word not by my circumstances. See Col 1:24)*

2 Tim 2:10 This gives me more than enough reason not to quit. I desire for everyone to discover the fact that the life of their [1]design is redeemed in Christ Jesus; this is the timeless intent of God. *(The word [1]eklegomai, ek, source, origin, and legomai from logos, word, thus the life of our design.)*

2 Tim 2:11 The logic of God endorses our faith: we were included in his death and are therefore equally included in his resurrection.

2 Tim 2:12 Whenever we face suffering, we already know that we co-reign with him; the Christ-life rules. *(Sufferings do not distract us, neither do they contradict our joint position with him in the throne room!)* If we [1]contradict ourselves *(behave unlike ourselves)*, he will contradict us and prove us wrong! *(The word [1]arneomai means to contradict.)*

2 Tim 2:13 Our unbelief does not change what God believes; he cannot contradict himself! *(See Rom 3:3,4 What we believe about God does not define him; God's faith defines us. God cannot be untrue to himself!)*

Why spend your energy and labour for a reward that leaves you frustrated and empty? Isaiah 55:2. The law of liberty takes doing beyond duty. This liberating lifestyle expresses the energy of God in you naturally, where you sense that instead of getting tired and weary your strength taps into another source where you mount up with wings like an eagle. Isa 40:31.

The law of liberty and spontaneity releases a much greater motivational

143

incentive, than what any law based on fear or reward or moral obligation could do. Under this law, walking the second mile becomes the natural thing to do! The teaching of the truth brings forth spontaneity. If what you hear only appeals to your willpower and leaves you feeling guilty and frustrated, you are listening to the wrong Gospel!

This same law of love is powerfully demonstrated in the area of finances: Paul boasts about the churches in Macedonia how, "in a severe test of affliction, their abundance of joy and their extreme poverty have overflowed in a wealth of liberality. For they gave according to their means, and beyond their means, of their own free will, begging us earnestly for the favor of partaking in the relief of the saints. *(In modern churches it is often the preacher begging his congregation to give!)* Now as you excel in everything, in faith, in utterance, in knowledge, in all earnestness and in your love for us, see that you excel in this gracious work also." 2 Cor 8:1-7.

Grace defines our lives. Many well-meaning believers are living ineffective and fruitless lives, having become blind and shortsighted to the wealth that is within them. Seeing energizes and equips the believer. 2 Peter 1:8,9. Ignorance and wrong teaching neutralizes people and empowers deception. Any teaching that emphasizes the responsibility and contribution of the individual to do things in order to gain God's approval, keeps the person in bondage. This type of teaching sustains a sin consciousness and keeps a person enslaved to feelings of inferiority and guilt. The merit of God's favor, love, approval and presence, does not lie in the degree of someone's crisis or even in the effort of man to justify or qualify himself; but in realizing the value God has placed upon us, while we were yet sinners.

God cannot divorce himself from his image and likeness in man. You are irreplaceable; you are his original thought; you occupy the mind of God for all eternity! We are dealing with an eternal romance that can never be exhausted!

CONCLUSION

You are free to live the life God imagines for you. We are designed to live not by bread alone but by the expression of God's opinion of us, "by the complete word that proceeds from the mouth of God." Mathew 4:4. The Hebrew word, kol, is often translated, "man shall live by "every" word that proceeds from the mouth of God, but it really means the "complete" word. Jesus is the word of God in its most complete context. God's authentic thought is the blueprint of your life, mirrored and redeemed in Jesus Christ.

In the natural, physical realm, "we possess nothing but the moment; polish it like a jewel" E. Goudge. Appreciation polishes the moment and brings out the brilliance of every hidden beauty. Within the moment there lies a potential energy that can either harm or bless you. Cultivate the habit to embrace beauty. Moments store energy in memory. Learn how to extract the vital energy. Appreciation, admiration and affection reflect virtue and value; this is the essence of life.

Let the light of God's favor dispel the negative of failure. A sense of failure will poison your system and paralyze your faith. Encourage yourself in God. 'The communication of your faith will promote the knowledge of all the good that is in you in Christ Jesus; or: Ignite the fellowship of your faith by acknowledging every good thing that is in you in Christ.' Philemon verse 6.

Identify the times of breakthrough and victory. Bring to mind those images of joy. Remember his divine protection and provision. Remind yourself what it feels like to be totally overwhelmed by God's goodness and presence. Spiritual and eternal realities always put physical and time-related experiences into proper perspective.

Surround yourself with gratitude; this makes it impossible for self-pity, anger or disappointment to gain any ground. Celebrate the success of the cross. Redemption is valid.

God gave Jesus a Name that is above every other name, authority, power or principality. His reputation to save and to heal exceeds the reputation of alcoholism, drug-addiction, AIDS, cancer or any disease or bondage, to kill and destroy.

Hold fast to the confession of your faith:
I am spirit.
I have a healthy body.
I am blessed with a sound and intelligent mind.
My life makes dynamic sense.

I believe that God is and I am.
I am God's idea and his delight!
His image and likeness reflects in me.
In the mirror of my spirit I see his face.
I see also every man included in his embrace.
I am born of him,
I am one with him.
He is my origin and my true father.
I am indeed his offspring, the product of his intimate imagination.
I was with him in the beginning.
He is also the conclusion of my life and my eternal destiny.
From him and through him and unto him are all things.

A BUILDING WITHOUT WALLS
Does the rain have a Father?
Who begot the drops of dew?
Who birthed the morning?
Caused the dawn to know its place?
Have you comprehended the expanses of the earth?
Have you comprehended their origin?

He knows you by name
His design is his claim
He boldly declares, "Measure Me"
Have you measured your heart?
Have you measured the volume of your being?
He has chosen you to accommodate the fullness of his dream

Have you comprehended? He is at home within your heart,
A dwelling built within you without walls.
Take my love to its conclusion.
Take my love to every man,
Count the stars, count the sand
Measure the nations in my Hand,
Come on now, measure me
I fulfill your eternity. (ANTHEA - Acts Team 1986-1990)

No grander thought can occupy my mind
than the thought that I am the fruit and object of God's thought.

I experience and express the essence of all virtue -
oneness with my Origin.
This is an amazing thing
that within my awareness of You

there exists an immediate sense
of belonging
and being
one with You.

I salute You kindly
Author of my life,
Master of my destiny.

God hovers over your life
with patient anticipation.

God is what life is all about.
If God doesn't make sense
then nothing else does.
Man was designed for the presence of God,
not for his absence.

He holds all things together by the word of his power. Heb 1:3 We have
our beginning and our being in him. He is the force of the universe, sustaining everything that exists by his eternal utterance! Jesus is the radiant
and flawless expression of the person of God. He makes the glory (*doxa,
intent*) of God visible and exemplifies the character and every attribute of
God in human form. *(Gen 1:26, 27)* This powerful final utterance of God
(the incarnation revealing our sonship) is the vehicle that carries the weight
of the universe. What he communicates is the central theme of everything that exists. The content of his message celebrates the fact that God
took it upon himself to successfully cleanse and acquit humankind. The
man Jesus is now his right hand of power, the executive authority seated
in the boundless measure of his majesty. He occupies the highest seat of
dominion to endorse our innocence! His throne is established upon our
innocence. *("Having accomplished purification of sins, he sat down.")*
.
In him we live and move and have our being.
We are indeed his offspring. [Paul quoting a Greek philosopher, Aratus,
in Acts 17.]

God is not a convenient crutch to lean on from time to time.
He is your life…to ignore him is to betray yourself.

Saint Augustine born in 354 in North Africa said:
"And Who is that God but our God,
the God who made heaven and earth, who filled them

because it was by filling them with himself
that he has made them."

Six hundred years ago, Dame Julian said, "He is our clothing that wraps us and winds us about, embraces us and all encloses us, for love... remain in this and you shall know more of the same... without end."

Albert Einstein (1879-1955) once said: "I am a Jew, but the glorious picture of the Nazarene made an overwhelming impression on me. No one has expressed himself so divine as he did. There is only one place on this earth where there is no darkness. That is in the person of Christ. In him God has placed himself in the plainest possible way right in front of us"

Never abandon Hope. Hope sees a future. Hope sees the harvest.
Hope understands the virtue of patience, and employs time as its friend and partner.

I stood on a commercial property a while ago and began to dream what a developer could do should he enjoy unrestricted access to it, and unlimited resources!
Imagine what God could do in and through you with your permission!

Imagine the music that lies dormant in one violin.
Play me Lord!

I dreamt one night that I was in a lecture room taking down the following notes:

A memory has 3 ingredients:
- the actual event or thought
- my reaction or specific experience of the event and
- the effect the memory continues to have in my life.

The event cannot be wished away; it is historic and on record, but the effect that it has on me now, can be challenged.

The greatest thrill and joy in my life is to experience divine feedback from the thoughts God inspires in me. There is nothing that overwhelms and fulfills me more than the awareness of his presence in me. "He is indeed my exceeding great reward". At the same time I struggle with the frustration of having to deal with interruptions to this sacred encounter. Not necessarily the interruptions of people and circumstances, but often my own temperament seemed to contradict and spoil my wonderful awareness and feelings of bliss. I am amazed that one can enjoy a most wonderful encounter with God, an overwhelming awareness of his presence and indwelling, and moments later to find oneself getting irritated or annoyed with something or someone. I still respond in anger or worry when I know that something can only upset me with my permission. It seems to me that I am stuck with some stupid habits. Especially when I feel tired and under pressure, I tend to over-react and then to take it out on the very people I care for most. Eish!

The "three memory ingredients" in my dream made me realize that one's mind is much like a computer, and that many "memory files" could still have a conscious or even sub-conscious effect on one's life. Old habits then feed off these memories and trigger various reactions that could trap one in frustration and embarrassment. Habits can either be the result of genetically transmitted traits or the effect of decisions and thought-patterns developed over time. Paul says that we have weapons that are powerfully employed to demolish every stronghold. A stronghold suggests a mindset that is triggered into action often by a single thought! The revelation of the consequence of the obedience of Christ is the sharp edge of the spear-point with which we arrest every thought and thus demolish every stronghold. 2 Cor 10:4-5. The KJV or NAS translates this verse correctly, "the obedience of Christ is the key, not, "to obey Christ" like many translations suggest! If your victory had anything to do with your obedience then then your willpower or decision could save you; then you wouldn't need a Savior! See Rom 3:27

To know the truth is to overcome an already defeated foe. The anti-virus protection on your PC is a good example of the filter-effect of the word of truth. Heb 4:12. There exists no sin or evil that can escape the scrutiny of the consequence of his obedience in my confession and conscience.

I am convinced that the only effective way to address this problem with confidence and authority, is to consider the two "out of all proportion to man's historic experience" realities: (Rom 5:17-19)

1/ As a living spirit I am designed in the image and likeness of a perfect God. He loves me and is not embarrassed about me. His image and likeness is preserved in my spirit, just like the watermark in a paper note; everything else about me is subject to change.

2/ The death and resurrection of Jesus on humanity's behalf remains the eternal witness to man's acquittal. He successfully rescued his image and likeness in me!

There is nothing wrong with me because there is nothing wrong with my design or my redemption!It is our thinking that was wrong! Isa 55:8-11.

Meditating on these truths brings immediate victory. Faith awakens and releases the love of God and then enables us to forgive ourselves, and those who have sinned against us. Any ground for guilt, disappointment, anger or even depression is effectively removed. We must determine to see ourselves exclusively in the light of God's opinion: "in your light do we see the light!" Ps 36:9. Light always dispels darkness. A renewed mind conquers the space that was previously occupied by worthless pursuits.

Overcoming the effect of negative memories and bad habits become real trophies in one's life. A point of weakness now becomes strength, instead of fear, a sense of positive expectation rules.

And while, like an eagle, I sit quietly on the edge of a cliff, the previous flight remains fresh in my mind. The adrenaline is already bursting with expectation for the next adventure. The Hebrew word 'KAWVA' in Isaiah 40 '…wait upon the Lord' literally means to be intertwined. Now life becomes really meaningful. It is not necessary to ever so often faint with frustration. Knowing the secret of soaring like an eagle makes one comfortable with any pace.

Heb10:1 For the law presented to us a faint shadow, outlining the promise of the blessings anticipated in the coming of Christ, even detailing its future significance. The mere sketch however, could never be confused with the actual object that it represented. The annual sacrificial rites as shadow of the eventual object would always leave the worshipper feeling inadequate and be a reminder year after year of the sinfulness of man. Heb 10:2 If it was possible to present the perfect offering that had the power to success-fully remove any trace of a sin-consciousness, then the sacrificial system would surely cease to be relevant. *(The measure of success must be such that God's affirmation of our innocence would be reflected. [See Heb 10:17])* Heb 10:3 But in the very repetition of these ritual sacrifices the awareness of guilt is reinforced rather than removed.

Heb 10:19 Brethren, this means that through what the blood of Jesus communicates and represents, we are now welcome to access this ulti-mate place of sacred encounter with unashamed confidence.

Heb 10:20 A brand new way of life has been introduced. Because of his flesh torn on the cross *(our own flesh can no longer be a valid excuse to interrupt the expression of the life of our design)*.

Heb 10:21 We have a High Priest in the house!

Heb 10:22 We are free to approach him with absolute confidence, fully per-suaded in our hearts that nothing can any longer separate us from him. We are invited to draw near now! We are thoroughly cleansed with no trace of sin's stains on our conscience or conduct. The sprinkled blood purges our inner thought-patterns; our bodies also are bathed in clean water. *(Our behavior bears witness to this.)*

Heb 10:23 Our conversation echoes his persuasion; his faithfulness backs his promises. *(His integrity inspires our confession.)*

Heb 4:11 Let us therefore be prompt to understand and fully appropriate that rest and not fall again into the same trap that snared Israel in unbelief. (The believed a lie about themselves, Num 13:33)

Heb 4:12 The message that God spoke to us in Christ is the most life giv-ing and dynamic influence in us, cutting like a surgeon's scalpel, sharper than a soldier's sword, piercing to the deepest core of human conscience to the dividing of soul and spirit; ending the dominance of the sense realm and its neutralizing effect upon the human spirit. In this way man's spirit is freed to become the ruling influence again in the thoughts and inten-tions of the heart. The scrutiny of this word detects every possible disease, discerning the body's deepest secrets where joint and bone-marrow meet. *(The moment we cease from our own efforts to justify ourselves, by yielding to the integrity of the message that announces the success of the Cross, God's word is triggered into action. What God spoke to us in sonship (the incarnation), radiates his image and likeness in our redeemed innocence. [Heb 1:1-3] This word power-fully penetrates and impacts our whole being; body, soul and spirit.)* Heb 4:13 The whole person is thoroughly exposed to his scrutinizing gaze. Every creature's original form is on record in the Word. *(Representing God's desire to display his image and likeness in man.)*

Heb 4:14 In the message of the incarnation we have Jesus the Son of God representing humanity in the highest place of spiritual authority. That which God has spoken to us in him is his final word. It is echoed now in the declaration of our confession.

Heb 4:15 As High Priest he fully identifies with us in the context of our frail human lives. Having subjected it to close scrutiny, he proved that the human frame was master over sin. His sympathy with us is not to be seen as excusing weaknesses that are the result of a faulty design, but rather as a trophy to humanity. *(He is not an example for us but of us.)*

Heb 4:16 For this reason we can approach the authoritative throne of grace with bold utterance. We are welcome there in his embrace, and are [1]reinforced with immediate effect in times of trouble. *(The word, [1]**boetheia**, means to be reinforced, specifically a rope or chain for frapping a vessel in a storm.)*

WINTER– The womb of new beginnings.

This letter was the last conversation I had with my mother before she passed away in February 2003:

I will endeavor to learn from the seasons;

That is to allow winter to run its course in my life with dignity,

Not regretting the loss of leaves.

Rather embracing the chance to gather secret strength from my roots:

A well of life that remains an invincible testimony to an inevitable turn in season.

Together with the early and the latter rain we will again celebrate the song of spring.

In your presence even the night is light. I welcome the wilderness. The winter finds me sheltered in your joy.

"Standing before the solid oak table, which was sacred to his clock alone, his heart beat high with joy at what he saw. No one else would have seen anything but a confused jumble of mechanism; but Isaac saw his clock, as it would be. He saw the accomplished thing. Like all creators he knew well that strange feeling of movement within the spirit, comparable only to the first movement of the child within the womb, which causes the victim to say perhaps with excitement, perhaps with exasperation or exhaustion, "there is a new poem, a new picture, a new symphony coming, heaven help me!" The complete picture lived already in his mind, visualized down to the last scale on the glittering silver fish at 12 o'clock. Isaac had the kind of mind that delights to collect the pretty coloured fragments of old legends that lie about the floor of the world for children to pick up. As man and craftsman he knew that he would touch the height of his being with the making of this clock. His heart beat fast and music chimed in his head. He covered the lovely thing with a cloth and turned away. It was hard to leave it even though there was nothing under the cloth except a medley of bits of metal and some oily rags. E. Goudge - The Dean's Watch.

God touched the height of his Being when he made me!

"Even the darkness is not dark to Thee; the night is bright as the day, for darkness is as light with Thee. For Thou didst form my inward parts, Thou didst knit me together in my mother's womb. I praise Thee for I am awesome and wonderfully made. Wonderful are Thy works! Thou knowest me so well. My frame was not hidden from Thee when I was being made in secret, intricately wrought in the depths of the earth. Thy eyes beheld my unformed substance. In Thy book were written, every one of them, the days that were formed for me, when as yet there were none of them. How precious to me are Thy thoughts O God! How vast is the sum total of them! If I would count them they are more than the sand; my years would have to equal yours.

When I awake, I am still with Thee. Ps 139:12-18.

DEALING WITH GRIEF

The following is an extract from a letter I wrote to a very dear friend who lost her husband in a tragic accident in 2002:

It is sometimes so difficult for us to really understand another's pain and agony. Grief at times must be the ultimate challenge to sanity. Yet wounds, even the most severe, heal. We are designed with such an amazing ability to absorb life's calamities.

Death makes so little sense, especially its finality and its awful suddenness. But we must believe that life will again make sense, and its wonderful sense will abolish the horror of grief now.

My friend broke his pelvis in a motorbike accident and had to lie in traction for six weeks. The amazing thing about the body is its frailty and yet, at the same time, its resilience and ability to bounce back. It literally is just a matter of hanging in there.

In Rick's case, it was impossible to operate, because the bone was shattered in a thousand pieces, so to hang in traction was the only solution. I think that sometimes our minds too need to be hung in traction as it were, it might be most uncomfortable, but given time and steadfastness, it will heal. In the process of 'hanging in' it is such a relief to know a place of escape in God's loving embrace. His overwhelming nearness is your portion now, and he lifts you into new perspective. Isa 40:27-31

God and life does not expect you to always find instant answers to burning questions, but at least to access thought that will nourish you now with comfort in all your affliction. The thought of our oneness with God and with one another is such a wonderful inspiration and comfort. He is the fountainhead within you. All your springs of joy are in him.

In every "natural" thing that happens to us, daily, in small things

and also from time to time in the big things like death and birth,

there comes with it, a unique and infinite opportunity to experience God in a "supernatural" way!

I believe that God desires to show himself strong on your behalf. I am confident that the substance of your make-up and your roots in him will continue to sustain you. He who said, "Let light shine out of darkness", has shone into our hearts!

God is ready to anoint you in a new way with a wisdom that comes from above and bursts forth from within.

FACING CRISIS WITH CONFIDENCE

I wrote the following in a time of severe financial crisis during the winter of 2002:

Faith confidence draws on a resource of strength and resolve bigger than the challenge.

It is a powerful release of inner energy that flows from a mind addicted to positive life; a mind that is exercised in the process of thought patterns consistent with the blueprint of our design as mirrored in the face of man's true genesis.

We are fashioned in the same mold, the expression of the same thought. Our Author's signature and invisible image is nowhere better preserved or displayed than in our inner consciousness. Our origin traces the very imagination of God. Every invention begins with an original thought; I am his original thought.

This state of mind liberates one to act and respond in total contrast to crisis: Joy takes charge. The most sober calculation one can make is a conclusion that always results in joy.

In every time- and space related experience there exists a reality of greater significance. A significance at hand, within the grasp of the individual. A reality that, once realized, can convert any negative energy into a force of light that dispels darkness effortlessly.

No experience, circumstance or person has what it takes to disqualify, humiliate, offend, or even upset you, without your permission.

Confidence equips you with an attitude that will attract solutions that will astound you!

I remember how Lydia and I would often during these times of severe challenge, get the children to help us prepare a feast with whatever we had to eat; even spending a last dime on a bottle of wine! We would celebrate a faith-feast in the midst of famine!

A LETTER TO THE LEADERS (2002)

Dear World Leader,

It is with the greatest respect for your honored position that I address this writing to you.

To be placed in a position of decision-making that could impact and even transform human history must be frightfully awesome.

Most of us believe that individually we play a small part in the process of democratic decision that ordain our leaders to represent our dreams for a society that will ultimately, even in its complex forms, reflect our most basic aspirations.

Should our mutual respect for one another be challenged, our highest moral value is at risk.

It is within this context I wish to quote these striking thoughts:

No man can live happily who regards himself alone,
Who turns everything to his own advantage.
One must live for another if one wishes to live for oneself.
True fiends are the whole world to one another,
And he that is a friend to himself is also a friend to mankind.
Seneca 4 BC – AD 65 Roman Philosopher

This would suggest that it is impossible to live a meaningful life as an individual at the expense of others.

You cannot truly regard yourself without a mutual regard for your fellow man as well as your Maker. The conclusion of all commandments remains, "to love the Lord your God with all your heart and all your mind and all your strength and to love your neighbor as you love yourself"

This would be an impossible task in the absence of realized value. To also love your enemy, is certainly the ultimate challenge under this law. Our ability to see value in another must be kindled, even if those values have become crusted over with corruption, fear, disappointment and hatred.

The human spirit, enlightened by the reflection of the Spirit of our Maker, continues to be the dominant force against corruption and all manner of darkness.

Suspicion and prejudice are overpowered by forgiveness, integrity and friendship. These are forces of light and life that can never be underestimated.

The greatest personal gain is to love and give without a thought for personal gain. Can you imagine a society where this attitude rules? Not even war can be more imposing.

I believe that the central focus of our education must again become a "drawing out of that which lies within us" (which is the literal meaning of the word "educate") rather than only a "putting in" of volumes of information.

Our mind, as a mental faculty, entertains thought and expresses emotion from one of two sources, the senses or the spirit. Spirit knowledge comes from within, while our senses can only relate to our external environment. Spirit knowledge is realized through resonance and faith (The word, "understand" in Greek is *sunieimi* which literally means a joint-knowledge, a flowing together as of two streams. Also the word for conscience: *suneidesis* from *sun* + *oida*, means a joint- seeing.)

Love, joy, peace, patience, kindness, goodness, integrity, humility and self-control, are not fragile, fading emotions, produced by willpower. They are powerful expressions of the soul; they are the fruit of spirit knowledge. These character qualities are not rewards for the most diligent and disciplined among us, neither are they mere "pie in the sky, wishful thinking" illusions. They reflect in fact the very nature of our design. They are our blueprint, the mirror image of our being. Window-shopping only teases one with dreams and desires beyond one's reach. Gazing into the mirror, however, reveals the essence of our redeemed nature, the image and likeness of God. 2 Corinthians 3:18. To strive to obtain love, peace and joy etc. or to pray to God to give us these qualities is wasted religious energy. To simply realize their presence within is what sets us free to be who we are.

The classic story of "The Ugly Duckling" is so appropriate; the mirror reflection reveals that we were swans all along. Also the lion cub in the movie 'The Lion King" reminds of the same truth: when he stares into the pool of water, his own reflection becomes the face of his father. Like the watermark on a paper note, our true self carries the exact imprint of God's character. This "watermark" parallel is also reflected in the seed concept. Every seed is engineered with all the genetic information of the species.

What ignites the life cycle and visible expression of the species is what matters. The fountain within us is released when we discover our common origin, revealed and redeemed in Christ. Our basic design and make-up originates from a common thought. Every invention begins with an original thought. In the core of our spirit our original design remains intact. Everything else about us can be challenged and changed, especially our mind, moods and circumstances.

To consider the image of God in a person, adds a value to the individual that exceeds any talent, skill or achievement. (Or disappointment for that matter.) Nothing is more rewarding than to discover the person in another person. Only discovering the person in oneself equals that.

'There is not a thought nor a feeling, not an act of beauty or nobility whereof man is capable,
But can find complete expression in the simplest, most ordinary life."
Maeterlinck

"A human being is like a work of art, the more it is admired, the more beautiful it grows, reflecting the gift of love, like light, back to the giver." Elizabeth Goudge

Ultimately a leader is called to serve his people. The greatest service that can be offered to mankind is not to make one person more and more dependent on another nor even to keep them dependent upon the charisma of the leadership and social structures they submit to, but to encourage and allow every individual to encounter the fountain within.

Discovering this wealth within is what liberates and empowers one to be an asset and not a liability. This alone will break the bonds of poverty, greed and corruption. The compulsion to take and have is replaced with a desire to share and be useful.

The awareness of who we really are and the greatness that dwells in us is out of all proportion to the illusion of lack and need.

The woman at the well was confronted with the realization that Jesus was more than a Jew and that she was more than a Samaritan. Suddenly she understood that all people indeed share the same origin. The fountain of living water was not distant from her, beyond her reach, but within her. Not any of her previous five marriages or even her religious tradition could quench her thirst. Not because she failed to meet "Mr. Perfect", or they failed to meet her expectation, but simply because of the fact that a partner or even traditional religious routine was never meant to complete her life.

Nothing and no one can equal the wealth someone discovers when one discovers one's Origin as the fountain of life. Here, there remains no partner, politics or past experience to blame or compete with, only a new life within you to discover, explore, enjoy and share. (The Gospel of John Chapter 4:4-34.)

Within this context, our mission in life is to help people discover the integrity of their authentic, individual value.

We are all the same, yet life finds a unique expression in each one of us that no one can repeat or compete with.

Great works do not always lie in our way,
But every moment we may do little ones excellently,
That is, with great love.
St Francis de Sales

From my heart to yours.

BEYOND DOUBT!

A cripple man, lame from his birth, sits in an audience one day where the words he hears arrest his attention. The thought that awakens in him is like rain upon dry soil. All the bitterness, anger and shame that imprisoned him from his earliest memories are challenged. A new, and yet in a strange way, a familiar voice, speaks in his heart.

Suddenly faith floods his face; he sees himself included in this message of love, hope and power. The God of the universe is graphically displayed in the camouflage of frail flesh. His dying on a cross redeemed a humanity fallen from the glory of their original design. This man Jesus, whom he heard various rumours about, represents the whole human race in his life, death and miraculous resurrection! The glory that Adam lost on mankind's behalf is redeemed again by the man, Jesus Christ! Is it possible that the same Spirit-power that raised him from the dead can now also restore his feet?

Like holding onto a life-line, he clung to every word Paul was speaking; and Paul, looking intently at him and seeing that he had faith to be made well, said in a loud voice, "Stand upright on your feet!" And he jumped up and walked!' Acts 14:8-10.

Faith is to your spirit what your senses are to your body. Faith sees and speaks! Paul preached in such a way, that many believed. Acts 14:1. Whatever holds you captive to an inferior lifestyle, crumbles in the light of the love of God, displayed in Jesus Christ as in a mirror. "And we all, with new understanding, see ourselves in him as in a mirror; thus we are changed from an inferior mindset to the revealed opinion of our true Origin." 2 Corinthians 3:18 (Greek: doxa, glory, lit. mindset or opinion) See also 2 Cor 5:14,16-21.

All of the Bible is about JESUS,
all of JESUS is about YOU!

A letter to Tanswell and Portia Davidse after the bombs:

It is such a joy and encouragement to hear your voice of faith!

What a statement you have made in your letter; I mean, if an act of terrorism can shake a city and a nation with fear, what will it take to shake a city and a nation with faith?!

It happened in the days of the Acts of the believers: "Paul spoke in such a way that many believed," Acts 14:1. "The place in which they prayed was shaken, and they were all filled with the Holy Spirit and spoke the word of God with boldness. Acts 4:31 "We cannot but speak of what we have seen and heard" Acts 4:20. "And the Word of God increased and the number of disciples were greatly multiplied!" Acts 6:7. A newly appointed deacon, Philip, went down to a city of Samaria, and proclaimed to them the Christ; and the multitudes with one accord (The revelation of Christ as the truth is in Jesus, reveals oneness and the inclusion of the multitudes!) gave heed to what was said by Philip, when they heard him and saw the signs which he did. For unclean spirits came out of many who were possessed, crying with a loud voice; and many who were paralysed or lame, were healed. So there was much joy in that city! Acts 8:5-8. (The act of terrorism left many injured and dead, and there was great fear and sorrow in the city.)

Imagine you empowered by God; you doing the works Jesus had done! When will we have enough money to hire a great evangelist to do it for us in our community?

"The righteousness that is of faith says, "Do not say in your heart, "Who will ascend into heaven to convince God to send Jesus down one more time (maybe if only for a 10 day crusade in my city?) Things might even get so bad that we lose our revelation of the resurrection, because righteousness by faith also says, "Do not say in your heart, "Who will descend into the abyss that is to bring Christ back from the dead!" But what does righteousness say? Righteousness by faith says!! "The WORD is near unto you! It is in your mouth and in your heart! The nearness of the word in your mouth and in your heart equals the very presence of Christ on earth; it equals the revelation of his resurrection from the dead! Righteousness by faith reveals that we were co-crucified; we co-died and that we were co-raised, and are now co-seated at the right hand of God to co-conquer the nations with him! Col 3:4 says every time Jesus is revealed, we are also co-revealed with him! In Acts 3 Peter does not apologize to the lame man about the absence of Jesus! He doesn't say, "Sorry sir, but you've missed Jesus by two months! He's in heaven now and you'll have to wait for his second coming which will only happen thousands of years from now! Instead he says, "The name Jesus means that what we have also includes you!" Peter declares with bold confidence that in the resurrection from the dead, God restored all things to mankind; the things of which all the prophets spoke when they proclaimed these days, "God having raised up his son, sent him to you first!" Here Jesus is revealed again in the lives of common uneducated men! Jesus is the restoration of all things. Acts 3.

Imagine your life touching another life with faith! Imagine you turning a city's sorrow into joy! Arise and shine for your light has come! Stand up in faith and make your voice heard! "Get thee up on a high mountain and lift up your voice with strength! "Anticipate rivers of living water gushing out of your innermost being!

"These men who have turned the world upside down have come here also!" Acts 17:6.

Paul never saw a weak gospel, he never considered a gospel of insignificant impact which would only appeal to a few individuals here and there! He didn't see its appeal reduced to a few desperate and lonely people who finally had no one else to turn to so they rather reluctantly and politely turned to Jesus, almost as if they were doing him a favor! Instead, Paul's mission was to make all men see, and to present all men in the full stature of Christ. Paul saw and proclaimed without hesitation or apology the gospel as the power of God, revealing God's righteousness from faith to faith. (He is the author and finisher of our faith; his faith ignites our faith) He declared the truth of our co-inclusion in Christ in such a way, that its appeal was like a mirror reflection. "With the open (unveiled) statement of the truth, we commend ourselves to every man's conscience" (Eph 3:9, Col 1:28, Rom 1:16,17, 2 Cor 3:18, 2 Cor 4:2)

I was reminded this morning of Romans 4, "Abraham did not misjudge (diakrino) the promise of God through unbelief! (There was no confusion in his judgment, even after years of contradiction, he was not influenced to make decisions based on circumstances, but what he knew to be true, continued to persuade him) That is why his faith was reckoned to him as righteousness. But the words, "It was reckoned to him" were written not for his sake alone but for ours also! This sounds like 2 Cor 4:13, "since we have the same spirit of faith as he had who wrote, "I believe and so I speak," we too believe and so we speak, knowing.....!" Paul is quoting David from Ps 116; verse 7 finds David speaking to himself, (You are faith's first audience!) "Return to your rest, o my soul, for the Lord has dealt bountifully with you! I believe and so I speak! (Some translations then say, "I am greatly afflicted" as if this was David's confession, the Hebrew actually says: I will sing loudly!)

God's faith, finds a voice in your mouth and a place in your heart that fully represents his eternal love dream realized it in Christ in the fullness of time!

My brother Hanri shared a lovely scripture with me last night from Heb 12:3, "consider him who endured such hostile contradiction..." The Greek word consider is the word analogitzomai which means to constantly, again and again come to the same logical conclusion!

Righteousness by faith sees the substance and the evidence of all we could ever anticipate concerning God's declaration of us, revealed, realized and fulfilled in Christ as in a mirror! Let's not wait for another day, another wave or another revelation or great idea, lets rather consider how to fan the flame within us and how to stir up one another and arouse one another by way of reminder! Let's consider what God decreed when Jesus cried out, "It is finished!"

"The zeal of the Lord will do it" Isa 9:7. Lets not confuse the zeal of God with zeal for God. Paul says of the Jews, "I bear them witness that they have a zeal for God, but it is not enlightened, for being ignorant of the righteousness that comes by faith, they continue to reason that their own effort to do something for God will be reckoned to them as righteousness" Rom 10:2-4.

The gospel reveals what God believes; it declares the love of God and the peace of God; it announces the joy of the Lord. The righteousness of God unveils what God did right inspite of what Adam or we did wrong!

The gospel does not reveal a potential you as in a display window; the gospel mirrors you in Christ! It cannot get any better than this! All of our conversation, our worship, our fellowship becomes a reflection of his final word, made flesh in Jesus, so that what is true in him is true in us! He has given us understanding to know him who is true and we are in him who is true! If we have received the testimony of man the testimony of God is greater! 1 John 2:7,8, 1 Jhn 5:9, 20.

God did not try and trick Ezekiel when he asked him if he thought that the dry bones he saw in a vision could possibly live again! I mean here Ezekiel is faced with the ultimate picture of defeat! A valley littered with dry bones of dead people! No-one survived! Ezekiel played it safe; we often do the same when faced with a seemingly impossible situation, "O Lord Thou knowest!" God did not say to Ezekiel, " Now stand back and watch me do it!" No! God said, "Ezekiel, prophesy to these dry bones! Eze 37:3 And he said to me, "Son of man, can these bones live?" And I answered, "O Lord GOD, thou knowest."

Eze 37:4 Again he said to me, "Prophesy to these bones, and say to them, O dry bones, hear the word of the LORD. Eze 37:5 Thus says the Lord GOD to these bones: Behold, I will cause breath to enter you, and you shall live. Eze 37:6 And I will lay sinews upon you, and will cause flesh to come upon you, and cover you with skin, and put breath in you, and you shall live; and you shall know that I am the LORD." Eze 37:7 So I prophesied as I was commanded; and as I prophesied, there was a noise, and behold, a rattling; and the bones came together, bone to its bone. Eze 37:8 And as I looked, there were sinews on them, and flesh had come upon them, and skin had covered them; but there was no breath in them. Eze 37:9 Then he said to me, "Prophesy to the breath, prophesy, son of man, and say to the breath, Thus says the Lord GOD: Come from the four winds, O breath, and breathe upon these slain, that they may live." Eze 37:10 So I prophesied as he commanded me, and the breath came into them, and they lived, and stood upon their feet, an exceedingly great host. Eze 37:11 Then he said to me, "Son of man, these bones are the whole house of Israel. Behold, they say, 'Our bones are dried up, and our hope is lost; we are clean cut off.' Eze 37:12 Therefore prophesy, and say to them, Thus says the Lord GOD: Behold, I will open your graves, and raise you from your graves, O my people; and I will bring you home into the land of Israel. Eze 37:13 And you shall know that I am the LORD, when I open your graves, and raise you from your graves, O my people. Eze 37:14 And I will put my Spirit within you, and you shall live, and I will place you in your own land; then you shall know that I, the LORD, have spoken, and I have done it, says the LORD."

"The first man Adam became a living being; the last Adam became a life giving spirit!" 1 Cor 15:45.

Peter's shadow radiated life. We are not just planet's, reflecting light, we are suns! We communicate virtue! When the woman touched the hem of his garment he was aware of virtue that flowed from him to her! We speak words that are not reduced to mere intellect, they impart life, combining spirit with spirit. 1 Cor 2:13.

Eph 4:14 The most dangerous life you can live is an ignorant one. You're left like an infant on a ship out of control in the waves and winds of the storms of life. The fall of the dice dictates while the deceptive teachings of men and their distracting tricks entertain.

Eph 4:15 [1]Love gives truth its voice. The conversation that [2]truth inspires creates the atmosphere wherein growth is both spontaneous and inevitable. The whole person is addressed in Christ who is the head of the body; he is the conclusion of God's communication with man. (*"Speaking the truth in love" is not only the preferred attitude in our every conversation, but the only option; where truth gives integrity to love, and love gives attraction to truth. Love,*

*[1]agape, comes from **ago**, to lead as a shepherd leads his sheep, and **pao**, to rest. God's rest celebrates our perfection; **agape** is to see the same value that God sees in every person. [2]Truth as it is mirrored in Christ [v 21].)*

Eph 4:16 [1]From him flows the original composition and detail of our design like words intertwined in poetry, ([1]like a conductor of music, [1]epichoregeo) they connect layer upon layer to complete the harmony, following the rhythm of his thoughts like footprints. Meanwhile the body thrives and pulsates with the energy of love. Each individual expression finds its complete measure there. *(The church is not a dismembered, dysfunctional body, but a fully functional, coordinated lover of people." — Rob Lacey)*

Eph 4:17 My most urgent appeal to you in the Lord is this: you have nothing in common with the folly of the empty-minded [1]masses; the days of conducting your lives and affairs in a meaningless way are over! *(The Gentiles, [1]ethnos, the masses of people who are walking in the vanity of their minds.)*

Eph 4:18 The life of their design seems foreign to them because their minds are darkened through a hardened heart ruled by ignorance. They are blinded by the illusion of the senses as their only reference, stubbornly wearing a blindfold in broad daylight. *(Hardness of heart is the result of a darkened understanding; a mind veiled through unbelief. [See 2 Cor 4:4])*

Eph 4:19 Having become conditioned to a life distanced from God; they are calloused in spirit, and are lust and greed driven; they have totally abandoned themselves to outrageous shameless living. (See Rom 1:19-23)

Eph 4:20 Of what total contrast is Christ!

Eph 4:21 It is not possible to study Christ in any other context; he is the incarnation, hear him resonate within you! The truth about you has its ultimate reference in Jesus. *("The truth as it is in Christ." He did not come to introduce a new compromised set of rules; he is not an example for us but of us!)*

Eph 4:22 Now you are free to strip off that old identity like a filthy worn-out garment. Lust corrupted you and cheated you into wearing it. *(Just like an actor who wore a cloak for a specific role he had to interpret; the fake identity is no longer appropriate!)*

Eph 4:23 Be renewed in your innermost mind! *(Pondering the truth about you as it is displayed in Christ)* will cause you to be completely reprogrammed in the way you think about yourself! *(Notice that Paul does not say, "Renew your minds!" This transformation happens in the spirit of your mind, awakened by truth on a much deeper level than a mere intellectual and academic consent. We often thought that we had to get information to drop from the head to the heart; but it is the other way around! Jesus says in John 7:37, "You believe that I am what the scriptures are all about, then you will discover that you are what I am all about, and rivers of living waters will gush out of your innermost being!)*

What helps me when I face difficult times is to know on a deeper level than what my senses are often aware of that my difficulties do not define me, and therefore I know that they cannot separate me from God or the life of my design

Many people everywhere have similar and perhaps worst situations to face than what you are facing right now!

All of us face contradictions and are often tempted to give the contradiction a stronger voice than what they deserve!

What God spoke to humanity in Christ is universally true for every single human life, whether we believe it or not, the truth of the full implication of God's love declared and demonstrated in Christ often remains veiled to us because our own circumstances seem to be more real.

God is not nearer to some than what he is to others; he is equally Emmanuel for every person on the planet! See Acts 17:27,28

It is really about two different dimensions we live in; the one is our sight, meaning our senses and what they perceive as our "reality", and the other is the realm of faith, and what God declares to be our truth that sets us free from the claim and dictate of the senses

When God calls things which are not as though they were it is because they are! They are more real and permanent that anything we perceive with the senses!

Paul says in 2 Cor 4:18...because we look not to the things that are seen but to the things that are unseen; for the things that are seen are transient, but the things that are unseen are eternal.

The Mirror reads: 2 Cor 4:18 We are not keeping any score of what seems so obvious to the senses in the natural realm, it is fleeting and irrelevant; it is the unseen eternal realm within us that has our full attention and captivates our gaze!

John 1:18 Until this moment God remained invisible to man; now the authentic begotten son, (monogenes, begotten only of God) the blueprint of man's design who represents the innermost being of God, the son who is in the bosom of the father, brings him into full view! He is the official authority qualified to announce God! (Official guide, eksegesato, from ek, preposition denoting source, and hegeomai, the strengthened form of ago, to lead as a shepherd leads his sheep; thus hegeomai means to be officially appointed in a position of authority. He is our guide who accurately declares and interprets the invisible God within us.)

2 Cor 3:18 The days of window-shopping are over! In him every face is unveiled. In gazing with wonder at the blueprint likeness of God displayed in human form we suddenly realize that we are looking at ourselves! Every feature of his image is mirrored in us! This is the most radical transformation engineered by the Spirit of the Lord; we are led from an inferior mind-set to the revealed endorsement of our authentic identity.

We walk by faith and not by sight... this is not a luxury option for some, this is the life of our design! 2 Cor 5:7

The Mirror Transation reads; 2 Cor 5:2 Facing pressure times the way we often do, makes us sigh with longing to exchange the skin-suit with the permanent splendor of the heavenly-suit.

2 Cor 5:3 In the meantime, whatever challenges we are facing in the meat-box, we know that we shall never be found naked; since we are already fully clothed with our heavenly identity in Christ in our inner person!

2 Cor 5:4 We are not complaining about our bodies, even though we are often aware of its frailties; instead we yearn to be overwhelmed with life. We know that every evidence of death even in our bodies, will dissolve into life!

2 Cor 5:5 God wired us this way; his Spirit already confirms within us the present evidence of eternity. We are eternal beings by design.

2 Cor 5:6 We are cheerfully courageous; knowing that our immediate address in our earthly bodies cannot distance us from the Lord, since we originate from him.

2 Cor 5:7 Faith is to our spirit what our senses are to our bodies; while the one engages with the fading and the fragile, the other celebrates perfection!

2 Cor 5:8 Our confidence stems from knowing that even though it might feel at times that we are merely reduced to flesh; our greater reality is that we are entwined in the Lord. He is our permanent abode! (The word, tharreo, means confident courage; eudokeo, means well done opinion; mallon, means prefer or rather; and ekdemeo, from ek, is a preposition that always denotes origin or source and demeo from deo, to bind, to wind, to tie, to knit; originating out of the body (we were knitted together in our mother's womb). In severe affliction one feels at times reduced to mere physical identity; but our persuasion is anchored in a greater opinion; the reality of our genesis in God and our union in him. The word, endemeo, means entwined, knitted together, tied in oneness. Yet at times

it almost feels strange to be trapped in this body especially when we are exposed to such abuse and suffering; one longs to then do the exchange and relocate to our permanent address, where our hearts already are; in the immediate embrace of the Lord.)

2 Cor 5:9 We are totally engaged in the loveliness of that which is of exceedingly great value; whether we are in a physical union with our bodies or a spiritual union with our source; it makes no difference to God's esteem of us! We are highly favored by the Lord. (The word, philotimeomai, comes from phileo, meaning dear, fondness; timay, meaning value, esteem; and einai from eimi, I am. The word, endemeo, means in union with, entwined; and ekdemeo means tied to our source.)

Draw from your source! He is within you and closer to you than your next breath!

Even youths shall faint and be weary, and young men shall fall exhausted; but they who engage their thoughts to [1]entwine with God's faith in them shall renew their strength, they shall mount up with wings like eagles, they shall run and not be weary, they shall walk and not faint! (The Hebrew word, kawa, means to entwine, to be platted together.) Isa 40:30,31.

James 1:3 Here is the secret: joy is not something you have to fake, it is the fruit of what your faith knows to be true about you! You know that the proof of your faith results in persuasion that remains constant in contradiction. Jam 1:4   *(Just like a mother hen patiently broods over her eggs,)* steadfastness provides you with a consistent environment, and so patience prevails and proves your perfection; how entirely whole you are and without any shortfall. Jam 1:5 The only thing you could possibly lack is wisdom. *(One might sometimes feel challenged beyond the point of sanity)* however, make your request in such a way that you draw directly from the [2]source *(not filtered through other opinions)*. God is the origin and author of wisdom; he [1]intertwines your thoughts with good judgment. His gifts are available to all, without regret. *(The word, [1]haplous, from ha, particle of union (hama, together with) + pleko, meaning to plait, braid, weave together. See Matthew 6:22, "If your eye is entwined with light your whole body will be full of light." Wisdom that comes from above remains unaffected by the contradictions of the senses. The word, [2]didomi, to give, to be the author or source of a thing — Wesley J. Perschbacher.)*

True worship is simply living in the overwhelming awareness of our oneness.

(Scriptures quoted: Mirror Bible unless otherwise indicated)

Other Books by Francois du Toit:

MIRROR BIBLE A selection of key New Testament texts paraphrased from the Greek   (A work in Progress)

DIVINE EMBRACE

THE LOGIC OF HIS LOVE

THE EAGLE STORY

DONE!

THE MYSTERY REVEALED

THE TRIUMPH OF FRIENDSHIP

www.mirrorword.net

Lightning Source UK Ltd.
Milton Keynes UK
UKHW020934220120
357413UK00011B/1001